Other Books b

CW00829336

BIRTH ANGELS BOOK OF DAYS ~ Vols. 1, 2, 3
Daily Wisdoms with the 72 Angels of the Tree of Life
Stone's Throw Publishing House (March, May & September 2014)

THE STORY OF LOVE & TRUTH
Stone's Throw Publishing House
Limited Handmade Edition (2007)
Illustrated Softcover Edition (2011)

BIRTH ANGELS ~ Fulfilling Your Life Purpose
with the 72 Angels of the Kabbalah
Andrews McMeel/Simon & Schuster (2004)
(acquired by Stone's Throw Publishing House 2013)
Greek edition: Asimakis Publishing, Athens, Greece (2014)
Czech edition: Barevny Svet s.r.o (2015)

YOU CAN WRITE SONG LYRICS
Writers Digest / F&W Publications (2001)

For permissions or information about author:
www.terahcox.com

Table of Contents

TERAH COX

Gratitudes

Since this volume is about relationship with others, I want to thank especially those who are the lights in my life – my nieces Bekah and Hannah, Aramis and Aden Zeno, goddaughters Lindy and Sara and their parents Art and Stacy, my sisters Cindy and Connie, friends Jodi Tomasso, Stacie and Shayne Florer, Arnie Roman, Tanya Leah, Chuck Pisa, Teri Barr and Amy Zachary. Deep appreciation also to the other stars in my personal galaxy – Paula Mooney, Lesley Majzlin, the Delzells, Honey Kirila, Davina Long, Paxton McAbee, Cathleen O'Connor, Saskia Shakin, Dave Robbins, Dominic Petrillo, Elizabeth Hepburn and Ken Appleman.

Many thanks to those who contributed their comments and stories to the introductory section of this volume – Stacie Florer, Jodi Tomasso, Paula Mooney, Chuck Pisa, Lindy Labriola, Grace, Helen and Lynn. And of course I continue to be so grateful to everyone who has supported the *Birth Angels Book of Days* project with your reviews, patronage, encouragement, word-of-heart-and-mouth, and more...

Aletheia Mystea, Amy Zachary, Anna Fyssa, Annie Lowe, Annie Shaw, Arnie Roman & Tanya Leah, Aura-Soma Koh, Barbara Lane, Beth Askew, Bobbie Martin, Bowie Yapp, Cathleen O'Connor, Chuck Pisa, Cindy Cox, Claudia Duchene, "Color Diva," Connie Kelley, Cornelius Chan, Crystal Yeung Kin Oi, Dan Koppel, Dana Ott, Darren Curtis, David P. Konowalchuk, Dionissia Kapa, Dominic Petrillo, Dorothy Barr, Dorothy Trottier, Efi Konida, Eleonora Kouvoutsaki, Elizabeth Hepburn, Ephrem Holdener, Everr Phoenix, Fan Michail Anurag, Fedra Tsiaka, Fai-Wen Voon, Garie Lo, Gigi Lee, Gittel Price, "Golden King," Harlina Aman, Hazel Ismail, Hazel, Yiu, Holly Koncz, Honey Kirila, Hung Chan, Katerina Palamidi, Kathy Boydstun, Imogene Drummond, Ishida Hiromi, Isobel Stamford, Jane Northup, Janice Tuchinsky, Jean Marzollo, Jeeval Kavassila, Jen Aly, Jenny Lou Murphy, Jodi Tomasso, Joyce Byrum, Judith Clements, Julie Ho, Karin Meury, Kaya & Christiane Muller, Kerry-Fleur Schleifer, Koya Yuen, Laura Gould, Leiola Reeder, Lenka Markova, Liliana Fantina, Lili Tan, Liliana Fantini, Lim Tet Soon, Lindy Labriola, Liz Sugg, Lokita Ghirarduzzi, Loretta Melancon, Lorraine Bordiuk, Lulu Bouchard, Madeleine Kay, Marc Sabin, Maria Macias, Margrit Hugi, Maria Crisci,

Maria Morana, Mary Carolyn Lawson, Mary Gracely, Michelle Wong, Miho Aladiah, Mike Booth, Ming Oi Go, Patrik Jonsson, Patty Harpenau, Paula Mooney, Pauline Lum, Pauline Van Oirschot, Rebecca Mitchell, Reina Pinel, Renata Cherestes, Rita Dulaney, RuoJian Yu, Sara Labriola, Saskia Shakin, Sarah Gallant, Shaleena MoonsStar, Sharon Etienne, Sharon Johnson, Siew Teng Lee, Sook Kheng, Stacie & Shayne Florer, Stacy & Art Labriola, Stephanie Delzell, Stephanie Sulger, Sue Heiferman, Stephanie Lodge, Tanya Leah, Teresa Peppard, Tina Wettengel, Tracey Robertson, Ulrike Lauber, Vassiliki Filippou, Vivian Wong, Wendy Cheng, Yokow XhN, Yvonne Foo, Yuta Kubareva.

I continue to feel special gratitude for the numerous tributaries of support from other aspects of my work as a writer, spiritual mentor and writing coach which have helped to support and inspire the intensive time I've needed for contemplation and co-creation with the Angelic Energies on this project: The Kleber family, Honey Kirila, Jodi Tomasso, Laurie Litwin, Rakesh Samani and Namaste Books (NYC); Archipelago, Country Touch, Passiflora, The Eclectic Collector, Winter Sun (NY); Kripalu Yoga Center (MA); Edenside Gallery, Promenade Gallery, Poor Richards (KY); Grovewood Gallery, Origami Ink, Malaprops Books, BB Barnes, Pisgah Inn, Carolina Creations, North Carolina Crafts Gallery, Crystal Visions, Local Color, Elements Spa, Quotations Café, Highland Books (NC); Raiford Gallery (GA); Spiral Circle (FL); Lyzart and Shaker Traditions (IL); Sacred Circle (VA); Angels Forever, Leap of Faith (WI); Art on Symmes, Gingko Gallery (OH); The Playful Garden (CA), Tree House Cottages Gallery (AR); Winnifred Byrne (OR).

Eternal gratitude to you all from the altar of my heart to yours! May your seasonal gatherings be loving and blessed...

~ Terah, October 2014

Preface

I was looking forward all year to doing this particular volume on "Relationship with Others," thinking it would be the easiest and most fun to do – but it has turned out to be the most challenging. I think this is because I've had to put into immediate practice in my relatings and relationships many of the Wisdoms as they were being co-created. Which meant, in the spirit of 'walking the talk,' I have had to 'walk' and 'talk' at the same time! During the time this volume was taking shape, an elderly friend with Alzheimer's whose care I manage from afar suddenly declined in health and was in and out of the hospital, which necessitated constant and often frustrating communications with numerous caregivers, doctors, nurses, therapists, social workers, and more. In addition to this was a rash of crises and counseling with friends and clients, plus my own increasing restlessness with long hours and months of intense writing and receiving. Add to all this the intermittent exhilaration of timely co-creative encounters and Spirit-filled conversations with friends, colleagues and "strangers" – and it seems that the Angels have been enacting the full spectrum of content in the Daily Wisdoms through everyone and everything around me. No sooner would a "daily" emerge than an issue or encounter would present itself for practical application!

During the journey of this project I have needed to curb a lot of my outer-world activities and socializations. Thus my relatings have been mostly with family, close friends and clients, whose varied personal stories of relationship dynamics I have mined, with their permission, for this Volume 4. Good friends and colleagues, Jodi Tomasso, Stacie Florer and Chuck Pisa, show up in a few of these. They utilize the Daily Wisdoms personally and professionally and often report uncanny correspondences between the day's Angel and their personal relatings and work events. Stacie often remarks how "perfect" the order and progression of Volumes 1-5 are. I finally really get that on a practical level with this Volume 4 as I have seen more and more how relationship with our inner Divine (Volume 1) helps to shape relationship with ourselves (Volume 2), our unique individuation through our work and soul purposes (Volume 3), and how these get put into practice in our personal relationships (Volume 4) and what we bring to our communities and the world (Volume 5).

It is often so much easier in life to 'talk' than 'walk,' to espouse than embody, to philosophize in the wings than to be on the front lines of interpersonal relating. As soon as the 'other' comes into the room, suddenly our own wills and ways have to move over a little to consider theirs. As soon as what you want is different than what I want, we need two TVs, two vacations or two sets of ingredients for the same dish. When you want to take a different route to get to the same place because of your different taste in scenery, does that mean then that we can't go together? If our life-songs are different, can we learn the harmony parts to sing along with each other – or must we go off into our own solo arias? And if one is sick or broken and needs attendance, how does the other bring caring without becoming depleted in order to be a regenerating presence of wholeness for oneself and the other?

These kinds of questions and more have been put to me in accelerated ways over these last few months especially. In a conversation about relationship challenges with my friend, Jodi, we finally got to this: we can't do this human life all by our human selves. Sometimes our relationships are just too hard. Sometimes we've done all we can and the wall is still there. We must have access to something that can help us to navigate the minefields of our reactive emotions and neutralize conflict without detonating! I think that "something" is faith. I don't mean the dogma of religion, but faith that we are part of "more than meets the eye." Faith that there are powers at work within and around us that are our allies – and that are always working for our greater good. In the language of the Angel Wisdoms, these powers within and among us are the grace-powers of love and truth that bring the quantum understanding, healing and reconciliation to our relatings when we "can't get there from here." By tapping these love-and-truth powers which compose our Divine-Human nature and our innermost resources, our lives and relationships can harness the energies of flow rather than force, of letting go rather than clinging to, of loving unconditionally rather than being held hostage to our needs and fears.

With love and truth within and among us, we can feel what there is to feel and not be afraid of our feelings or those of others as we realize that feelings are the breadcrumbs leading to our personal and mutual truths. We can learn to ask more of ourselves and each other in relationship, and not settle for so little just to keep from being alone. For no matter who and what comes and goes in our lives, with faith we come to know that truly, we are not alone here – even when we seem to be.

Love and Light,
Terah, October 2014

TERAH COX

The Gathering

* * *

We...
you and I
us and them – we all
greet...smile...talk...shout...whisper and dare
joyful...wondering...concerned...loving...
shy looks. And slowly, we thaw...
warm...embrace. And despite
whatever was or will be
we are all now-here
in this moment
where all our
power lies
to remedy
any past
and rewrite
every future.
And so we dance
laugh...share...forget
and remember – till
we catch each other's light
and absolutely sparkle together!

~ Terah Cox

TERAH COX

Introduction

This fourth volume of the **Book of Days** features Daily Wisdoms with the 72 Angels about our relationships with others, especially our partners, families, friends and peers. During this time of year with holidays and family gatherings, our relatings with those in our intimate circles are often the most poignant and sometimes the most challenging. Memories abound – and wishes for things in the past to have been different color our experiences with each other in the present. There is perhaps no time of year when our emotional energies are more intensified, and thus when we most need – and are most able – to heal and come closer to each other, if we dare. If we can see the sameness of heart underneath our differences – that we all desire to love and be loved and to have a meaningful, worthwhile life – then perhaps we can consider that although our feet may need to take different roads, our hearts are all headed to the same places!

How we are with others is a reflection of how we are with ourselves. If we have love, acceptance, compassion and forgiveness for ourselves, these will be almost effortless to extend to others. If we put our trust in our *own* resiliency to survive disappointment, betrayal or loss in relationship – rather than in trusting/expecting/demanding others to keep their promises and commitments to us – then we don't have to harbor long-term grudges, anger and resentment against those who at times, because of their own challenges, "fall from the grace" of our love and friendship. If we understand the things that bother us about others as "alerts" of what needs healing within ourselves, then we can see the other as a catalyst for our own self-realization, and be grateful.

The Angels tell us that the more we realize we are not separate from the Divine – that God is within and among us as the "Divine Stuff" we are made of – the more we will understand that in the bigger picture of our shared origin in the Oneness, we, as Divine-Human Beings, are not really separate from each other either. And yet, the gift of life and physical separateness gives us "time and space" to explore and cultivate to the nth degree each of our particular constellations of qualities and potentialities – and in doing so be compelling inspirations and support to each other.

As deeply as some of these dynamics are explored in the Wisdoms, many of the mysteries about ourselves and each other wait in the wings of our ability to receive. Just as the patterns of star constellations are defined by those particular stars that star-gazers have been able to see – there are so many more things to see about ourselves and each other that we won't see until we tap into the higher capabilities of our "inner resources." In the meantime, everything between us is a clue, a pointer, a mirror to the mysteries of ourselves, each other and all of life.

The Angels tell us that on a soul level we already know the mystery and possess the treasure. And so perhaps life is just a great game of hide and seek between soul and matter and the clues that lead us to find what is already here. And perhaps we shall even see that each clue, which we thought was only a breadcrumb, is made of the same ingredients as the whole loaf we are seeking. If we can love the individualities of ourselves and each other within the whole, we will come to see and feel, as William Blake said, "eternity in a wildflower" as the One in all and the All in one that we each are.

Thine Own Self...Unto Others

As many spiritual and therapeutic traditions tell us, our relatings with others mirror relationship with ourselves. Likewise, the Angels tell us again and again that if we have love and compassion for ourselves, we will know how to extend these to each other. The model for self-love is within us, in the way we are loved by the Divine that dwells within our hearts and souls. Our first and primary relationship is the one between our co-dwelling Divine and Human aspects – and it is this relationship that is amplified by the Angels as aspects of the Divine within our humanity. Our inner Divinity is the "invisible other" that teaches us how to be with the visible others who are our loved ones, family, friends, peers and all.

As the Angelic Energies shed their 72 different *angles* of light on our relatings and relationships, recurring themes proliferate throughout – some of which are:

Don't ever think you know all there is to know about the other. Everyone, without exception, is always growing and evolving – even if they seem to be still as a stone! And it is our interest in each other which helps to draw us forth and make us even more interesting. Often in longtime partnerships and friendships, we stop asking each other questions and listening for the answers. On the one hand, familiarity and seeming sameness are comforting; on the other hand, ceasing to explore the other's thoughts, feelings and ideas can cause our hearts to close off, our minds to dull and our mutual vibrancy to wane in each other's presence. As the Angel IAH-HEL says, true knowing is not about how much we know but how deeply we know. In that light, there is no end to what can become knowable and newly invigorating between us.

The only control we ever have over anyone else is through love. We cannot make someone be or act the way we think they should, for our good or their own. This recalls that old cliché about how "we can lead a horse to water, but we can't make him drink" – or "we can teach them, but we can't make them learn." We can give our children all the advantages and opportunities in the world, but we can't make them be good people or do good things. We cannot take what can only be given in a relationship and think even for a moment that we really possess it. Individual soul purposes and agendas in life are paramount – however, some people's agendas are beyond our ability to make sense of them! But love is the compositional creation energy of life, and as such has the beginning and final say in all things and beings. As the Angel JELIEL says,

> "The only truly transformative power that you possess to change another is love – but the change will be what is true and right for them. When you extend love to another through the _feelings_ or _actions_ of acceptance, compassion and forgiveness, you surround them with love's creation energy and the power to tap it if they so desire. Once love's presence has been amplified by your grace in giving it, love is like water – taking the shape of whatever it fills, and filling the invisible and seemingly impenetrable spaces where love has been forgotten. But know that as love seeps down into the roots of a person to bring nourishment and life, you may not see the fruit until their own season of ripening is at hand."

Only love knows the whole truth about a person. Whatever "truth" we hold in our minds about another is only a partial truth without love, because love sees our totality both in the eternal and in time. As the French writer Voltaire conveyed often in his satires, such as *Micromegas*, as well as in his criticism of the Academie Francaise in the 1700's, just because we can't see something doesn't mean that it doesn't exist. Or similarly in *The Little Prince*, by Saint-Exupery, "It is only with the heart that one can see rightly; what is essential is invisible to the eye." More of who we are is always on its way from within us into outer expression. Those who love us can see our potential – and even inspire it to emerge. Others see only what they're able to see, in large part due to what they cannot yet see about themselves. It is important to realize, however, that if we fall in love with potential – rather than the actuality of the person in the now – then in the ongoing now they may feel that they are not enough for us. And indeed, as they are now, they are not enough because we are in love with who they might be instead of who they are.

We have the power to not only affect, but effect each other. Our relationships are the greatest outer influences in our lives. We can give each other a sense of belonging, encourage our mutual dreams and purposes and help to inspire each other into self-realization – or not. But we can also be affected positively by relatings that seem to be negating. Rather than doing battle with or trying to "teach" the person who is not meeting our expectations of caring and consideration, we can cultivate a new level of self-sovereignty. By learning to embrace ourselves whenever someone else can't or won't, we cultivate core emotional strength and resiliency that can carry us through our greatest challenges.

"Hurt people hurt people." While I was working on one of the Angel Wisdoms about healing, I saw Jamie Lee

Curtis say this in a Facebook video post on bullying. Such a wonderfully succinct way to remind us how much hurt the "hurters" must be harboring that would cause them to intentionally or even unintentionally hurt others. She went on to suggest that what the bully really needs is a hug! And yet sometimes when the person doing the hurt receives love back they resist it because they can't bear the pain of how much they need it. In the meantime, we can use the hurts that come our way as examples of what not to be or do – rather than reacting to them in kind or collaborating in their hurt against us by letting our self-worth be diminished. Our refusal to receive the hurt causes the hurt to be "returned to sender," so that the opportunity for healing goes back to the source where it is needed.

The people who hurt us the most are often our greatest teachers. We are drawn to each other for both pleasure and pain – for not only what feels good and comforting and gives us a sense of belonging, but also for what we need to heal and learn. As the Angels put it, someone who "rubs us the wrong way" can be like the grain of sand in the oyster of our life which ultimately yields a shining pearl. We don't react to someone else's "stuff" unless it triggers our own. Abrasive dynamics are an accelerated means to slough off the barnacles of harbored hurts and hardened attitudes that turn into shields and walls of self-protection, which ultimately only "protect" us from being loved. Sometimes we pull people into our lives who are not our peers and who just don't have the capacity to love and support us in the way we desire. Our need to be loved triggers our tendency to try to mold whoever shows up into the ideal that we hold in our hearts and minds. By accepting oneself and the other, we can let go without judgment, and thereby extend the "grace-space" for each to be who we are and to grow in our own time – and perhaps free each of us to find "a better match."

The only battle worth winning is the one that cannot be fought. If you win all the battles and lose the war, then "what profiteth the score?" We don't win by fighting what we don't want, but by supporting what we do want – because only the latter generates life-affirming energies and outcomes. While it may be helpful to tell another what is not acceptable to us about their behavior, dwelling on it only instills shame and resentment. Better to move on to what we do want – and also ask the other what he or she wants, because their behavior may be an acting out of not getting something they need from us too.

"Do unto others as you would have them do unto you" is meant to protect us from perpetuating and compounding the pain that has been done to us by doing hurtful things to others. The deeper opportunity behind the "golden rule" is to help us change the past by changing any negative effect it has had on us. If we had terrible childhoods, we can re-parent and heal ourselves by parenting our own children better – rather than visiting upon them what we suffered. Treat someone who is unloving and disrespectful with love and respect, and the seeds of love and respect are planted within them that, in their own time of readiness, will begin to sprout.

We have the power to change the past by forgiving ourselves and each other in the present. A single forgiveness can redeem an entire family's history of recurring pain and heartache. Every time we allow someone's hurtful behavior to hurt us, their hurtful act is compounded by our receiving of it. When "the sins of the fathers are visited upon the children," and the children are compromised and even defeated by them, the "sins" get heavier and heavier with the accumulation through the generations until "the sins of the fathers are the shackles worn by their children" (character dialogue from the television show NCIS on the day I was writing this!). Each generation has the choice to continue to carry those shackles or discard them. We can get a pretty good view of this in at least the three generations that are usually present in our families.

As the Angel HAZIEL says, *"Forgiveness is for giving you back to yourself."* By getting out from under the yoke of accumulated hurt, we take its power away and reclaim our own. On an energetic level, this begins to mitigate the effect and thus lighten the weight of the offense that started it all. Simply put, it's like stopping the ripples from a stone thrown into a pond. By making a stand as the new source of your own life-stream, the healing ripples back to the original source of hurt and begins to neutralize and even null its effect. Thus "the sins of the fathers are *redeemed* by the children." And ultimately we free not only ourselves but our whole family – some of whom may or may not be able to accept the freedom in the time and way we would wish for them. But in respect for the agendas of their own souls, that has to be okay.

If there were really any such thing as sin, it would be judgment. When we harbor fixed judgments about another, we effectively deny their growth in our presence. Life is about the evolution of the soul in the human vehicle both for the fulfillment of its purposes and potentialities and to root the Divine on Earth through Divine-Human beingness. When we judge another and hold that judgment unmoving within us, then we deny what the Divine Itself has given all of us – the fluidity of love and truth that we are made of which continually evolve us into more loving and true versions of ourselves – and as unique differentiations of the Divine on Earth within humanity. As the Angel HAHASIAH says, *"if you continually live with judgment of self or others, you are sentencing yourselves to life without love's parole."*

The heart is not just about feelings. When we refer to our hearts, we are most often talking about our feelings, or perhaps our "truth." The heart, in its depth and scope as our sacred heart, the "seat of our soul" in human life – is the bridge between the Divine as our eternal soul-being and the Human as our physical form in time. In addition to being the inner well from which we draw love, compassion and forgiveness – those attributes that we inherent from our Divine "parent" – the heart is the receiver and broadcaster of the soul and its purposes from our inner into our outer lives and relatings. As keeper of our personal truth, the heart is the source of our other great Divine-Human internal resources: intuition, insight, understanding, and the wisdom that is forged by combining our human knowledge and experience with the greater knowing and transformative powers of love.

Togetherness is only as strong and vibrant as the individuals who compose it. The dance of individuation and togetherness is the paradoxical "pas-de-deux" that we are here to dance with each other. In our relatings comes the possibility for the most profound fulfillment of all, which is to experience the fruition of individuation in the context of togetherness. As the Angel MIHAEL says, *"As you go toward and away, toward and away, you each gather diversity of experience to bring back into the relationship to enrich the oneness."* Therefore, relationship has a vested interested in the fulfillment of the individuals who compose it, as the individuals rely on the richness of relationship for comfort, support and inspiration.

"Where two or more are gathered, there shall I be." This phrase, which appears in different words and ways in various spiritual traditions, is repeated by the Angels again and again in illuminating our power to conjure the Divine and the eternal in time and place through relationship and co-creativity. Our gatherings with each other are meant to be opportunities for amplifying Divine Presence and conjuring infinite potential within the seeming limitations of matter and time. Often, however, we use our gatherings to press conformity and status quo. The deeper mystery of "where two are gathered" is also an echo of that first moment of eternity in which the original "cosmic cell" of Divine Oneness differentiated/multiplied into two, from which all Creation was ultimately born. This is the power that we as Divine-Human beings also have within us – to come together with each other to create and multiply more and more of ourselves through our own creations, and our creations' creations.

The diversity of humankind is a reflection of the Divine Oneness diversified into and as creation. The diversities in humankind are a direct result and reflection of the inherent diversity of God/the Divine/Allah/the Supreme Being – and all the different names that our differences call the Oneness from which we were created. It is the differentiation of the original Oneness into the many that is said to have brought about Creation. The why of this has been speculated upon probably since the first human loss of remembering our Divine parentage and Source – but we carry all the clues within the urges and desires of our humanity.

Just as we are urged to know ourselves better through the reflective eyes of the other upon us and what more we can become through our own creations, so it was and continues to be for the Divine Itself.

In the eternal-time-and-placelessness of "No-thingness" before "the Beginning," the Oneness could not fathom All that It was or what more it might become. Like white light that contains all the colors which remain invisible to the eye until the light is refracted, the Divine could not know Its own "contents" and capacities until It began to refract, or differentiate, Itself into distinct qualities of otherness. Through otherness, each aspect, or being, has the "space" to define, express and increase itself into the farthest possibilities of its own beingness. Like fire and water, as one they extinguish each other – but in physical separation they each have enormous powers to explore their paradoxical dual powers to create and destroy – the cycles of which expand creation *ad infinitum*. Thus, each different soul and Divine-Human being and thing in the "separateness nature" of physical life may come into greater and greater fulfillment of its unending potential.

Underneath our differences is a sameness of heart that allows us to come into unity from the inside, even while we are separate beings physically. We struggle with the concepts of separation and unity between us, as if unity is the more spiritually desirable concept, and separation a painful illusion. However, both separation and unity are sacred, and also possible, on Earth. For even though we exist in physical separateness here for cultivation of the Divine diversity within human diversity of form and expression – at any moment we can return to unity and the "Garden of Eden" that is the heart of God by returning to the sameness of heart within, between and among us all. Thus may we come to understand that...

We are all as leaves on one great Tree of Life. We are the many which express the One. As such, here we all are on the Divine Tree of our shared origin, each of us angling into the light and catching the wind with all our own unique ways and wonders. Yet not only do we lose sight of the Tree and forget the trunk and roots that sustain us – but we often treat the other leaves on the Tree not as our brothers and sisters, but our distant "poor relations" and even our enemies. In the greater reality beyond and despite our forgetting, however, not only is the tree sustaining all of us, but it takes all of us to express the fullness of the Tree's own potential – and also to bring the life-giving light that the Tree's roots need in order to keep sustaining us. And so to deprive or destroy another is ultimately to deprive and destroy our own selves. For truly, we cannot individually thrive on Earth unless we all thrive.

Healing and Helping

The Angel HAHAHEL (Mission) tells us that the trajectory of our life purpose is always moving from "karma to dharma" – essentially healing old issues and hurts and using our soul-lights and purposes to be of service to others. Karma is related to both the law of attraction and the law of balances that are both in play in the Biblical phrase "whatever ye sow, so shall ye reap." In other words, we get back what we put out, whatever goes around comes around, and so on. Karma is not about punishment, but the way in which the universe continually balances itself. In our personal lives and relatings, karma is composed of the accumulated and unresolved hurts we have caused to ourselves and others, and is life's way of giving us an opportunity to heal and "balance the scales" of cosmic justice by reestablishing personal equilibrium. Dharma is the expression of our soul purposes in service to others and the world at large – and it can take many forms throughout the course of our lives. You might say that karma is what we come in with that needs healing, and dharma is how we purpose our lifetime with helping – hopefully without taking one step forward and two steps back along the way!

For all the different things we think life is about and all the different things we do, it seems that this intertwined thread of healing and helping runs through them all. There are many ways, both personally and professionally, in which we heal ourselves and help each other to heal. Actually, as medical professionals and other healers agree, ultimately we do not actually heal each other. Rather it is the support we give and receive that helps to create an atmosphere in which healing can take place. Sometimes it is just the willingness of someone to sit with us in our pain that gives us the strength to bear and ultimately transform or overcome it.

We are often afraid of each other's pain because secretly we are afraid of our own. But pain is one of those "boogeymen" in life that casts a longer, scarier shadow the farther you stand away from it. The two-pronged prize of pain met head-and-heart-on is always humility and wisdom, topped off by a crown of self-sovereignty! For as the Angels say, saying yes to pain is also saying yes to the power we are endowed with from within to transform anything that comes at us into something light-bearing and life-affirming.

The Angels tell us that "the hand of God needs the heart of man to do Its work on Earth." Every act of love for another is the Divine loving the other through us, as us. Every helping hand and heart we give to another is the Divine reaching through our humanity to let us know that we are not alone here – that we are known and felt and watched over from within and between and among us helpers all, visible and invisible. Many of us have had guidance and "help" from the spiritual realms while awake and also while sleeping. I have experienced this many times – but there is one I'd like to share here because of the way it bridged the physical, spiritual and dream worlds.

Years ago I went through a time when a lot of stress was building up in my life, along with harbored emotional hurts. I started to experience symptoms around my physical heart – breathing discomfort, palpitations, twinges of pain and other things. Because heart disease runs in my family, and I had been previously diagnosed with a heart murmur and mitral valve prolapse, I was beginning to think maybe I should see a doctor – but I kept putting it off. One night after falling asleep, I had a dream in which I was "air-lifted" into a space vehicle of some kind to join a healing mission traveling to other worlds. I was to be part of the crew as one of the attendants to help bring people onboard wherever we landed to ready them for their healing treatment. That went on for awhile throughout the night, and then suddenly I found myself lying down with all the others, with a flying being (but no visibile wings!) hovering over me. I tried to protest that I was a helper, that he needed to heal the others instead. He only smiled a beautiful calming smile as he looked into my eyes, put his hand over my heart and said, "my dear, you have a hurt heart." In that instant, I knew he had seen the deeper pain, and all that was hurting in my heart surged and leaped to meet his touch as he drew the pain out of me. The pulling sensation was so powerful, so physical, that at the end of "the healing" I woke up. Amazingly, all the symptoms had disappeared – and long story short – never to return again in that magnitude, including the heart murmur and mitral valve condition. And there were other changes emotionally.

This dream-story has several layers of meaning, but three things in particular remain with me – one, that our hurt is known in the universe. We are not alone with our pain, unnoticed and unattended. Secondly, often we don't even know we're hurting until someone's touch begins to heal us. And thirdly, even those of us who feel called to be healers of others in our different ways also need to be healed. And we must allow this, even seek it out for ourselves, so that we may not only be present for the healing needs of others – but to also feel what it feels like to receive in this way and to allow others the experience of giving.

Family Constellations and Angel Prescriptions

The vibrational density and drama of physical life and relationship is so intense and compelling that remembering and drawing from the Divine that dwells within our Divine-Human beingness must be renewed continually. The 72 Angels are our inner touchstones for doing just that. I have seen again and again that by drawing on the Angelic Energies within and among us, our challenges and potentials in our relatings take on bigger-picture dimensions, as we take each other's behaviors less personally.

A couple of years ago a young woman, Grace, told me a wonderful story about how she and her husband finally healed a difficult time with their young son who was going through a stage of continually ignoring, disobeying and talking back to them over *everything*. This resulted in having to constantly discipline him in various ways by having his favorite things and activities taken away, which made him feel he was being treated unfairly and only caused more arguing and built-up anger and resentment in both him and his parents – especially Grace – since with home-schooling and other activities she was with him a good deal of the day. Over the course of a year he had become a pretty grumpy kid, and there was a general worn-out atmosphere in the household.

"Coincidentally," their son's Incarnation Angel is #33 YEHUIAH for Subordination to Higher Order, and his Heart Angel is #18 CALIEL for Justice. You could say he was acting out the Inversions (negative potential) of both of these by resisting his parents and their methods of justice for his disobedience. Finally, at their wit's end, Grace and her husband told him they were going to discuss what his punishment would be this time, and that they would tell him the next day. After he went to bed, they talked into the night about how to take a more spiritual approach in dealing with the issue. They finally had one of those "a-ha" epiphanies that gave them a whole new way to handle it. When he got up the next morning, they sat him down to discuss it and told him this was going to be a *permanent* punishment. As his eyes started to water, they told him: "Every time you get smart with us, every time you disobey or ignore or argue with us, you are going to get...a HUG! And we are going to hug you and hug you and hug you until you stop!" Startled, his teary eyes widened and he looked from one to the other of his parents, not sure what to do or think. They both smiled, and he started laughing as they gave him a pre-hug for what would likely be more to come. After a couple of weeks of "punishing" hugs (some of them embarrassingly public), he was a changed kid. His enthusiasm and joy had returned, he was doing better with his schoolwork, and he got to help decide how to organize his entertainment time, homework and family chores, and how family time would be spent. The whole family was changed as love, humor and lightness came back into their home. Interestingly, Grace's Incarnation Angel is #23 MELAHEL for Healing Capacity, and her Heart Angel is #40 YEIAZEL for Divine Consolation and Comfort.

Family members often share Birth Angels, and usually their Angels' Virtues and Inversions (positive and negative, or light and shadow, aspects) will be in plentiful expression! It's as if our shared Birth Angels hold clues to the purposes of our connections while at the same time giving us amplified resources for meeting our challenges and potentials together. Sometimes the challenges with certain family members are so great that we can't work out our issues directly with them for awhile. But looking at their behavior and our dynamics with them through the light of their Birth Angels, our own and any we share, helps to give us greater understanding. In the meantime, if we so desire, we can work with the family constellation of Birth Angels energetically until there's an opening to work directly.

It is important to understand that as difficult as the behavior of some is, they, and all of us, are working on soul issues that our human circumstances have provided a context for. We don't have to condone or perhaps even put up with others' behavior – but the opportunity here is to not take their behavior personally. Or, to use their behavior as a teachable moment for ourselves on any level it applies. This approach is what my friend Helen and her sister used to deal with some pretty "ornery" relations.

Helen's story. My friend Helen realized when she and her sister looked up the Birth Angels of certain chronically difficult members of her family that many of them were acting out mostly the Inversions of their Angels, uncannily so.

> "It gave my sister and me some relief to see that their actions were likely giving them an opportunity to explore the "flip side" of their more positive aspects. So we were able to consciously adjust our reaction to their shenanigans in such a way that their Birth Angels became a tool to strengthen our compassion, as well as to work with our own Birth Angels to tailor our responses to them in ways that would reinforce positive aspects and ways of relating instead of just reacting to them."

Stacie's story. As I've mentioned before, my friend, Stacie, has been working daily with the 72 Angels and Birth Angels materials for awhile now. She introduced her mother to the tradition, and they often work with the Angelic

Energies individually as well as together on personal and family issues. Stacie says,

> "Working together with my mother on the Birth Angels material has been instrumental in deepening my already great relationship with her. The daily wisdoms offer us a neutral place to discuss aspects of our daily experiences as they relate to our own relationship, and we are able to talk to each other about our sometimes different viewpoints of those experiences from a place of love and openness. We are now speaking the same energetic language, and that offers us more mobility and confidence in our individual understandings so that we can create new-to-us knowledge based on our shared perceptions. She also now understands more about my own soul tendencies, as well as I hers. That is a terrific gift in itself. It has allowed understanding where before in our relationship, there sometimes wasn't. We are both working on ourselves, and that has made our relationship even richer. We both now understand the importance of individuating and are delighted for each other's accomplishments in that vein. The Birth Angels material, especially the Daily Wisdoms, have helped facilitate that aspect of our mother-daughter relationship in all kinds of wonderful, unexpected ways."

Paula's story. And this is what Stacie's Mom, Paula, has to say about her experience with the Angels:

> "I've spent most of my life putting pieces of me into cubbyholes – daughter, student, wife, parent, caregiver, etc. – and splitting those assigned pieces into roles that would be acceptable and correct. Most of the time I was trying to remember that 'everything's not about me' and put focus on the comfort, well-being, and especially, approval of others (who were in their own cubbyholes). This all translated into worry, controlling behavior, and interference in others' business. It applied especially to my children...and they resisted! I've tried many things in an effort to deal with this issue, but until I started working with the Birth Angels it

consisted mostly of intellectual understanding and good intentions. Working with the Birth Angels daily readings has helped me to love and value myself enough to let go, act with love, and realize that when it comes to changing people, I can only change myself. It really is 'all about me' after all!"

One of the most difficult things for us to do in the context of our families is to suddenly stop participating in habitual group behavior that has long perpetuated family dysfunction. As hard as it is, and as much as everyone around you may resist and resent, standing up for your own truth and well-being in the middle of a tsunami of expectations, manipulations, resentment and conflict has the power to change everything in an instant.

Lynn's story. While working on the daily wisdom of CHAVAKIAH (Reconciliation) in this volume, I got a call from my friend Lynn one evening while she was sitting upset in the driveway of her mother's house after having rented a car and driven eight hours to be with her mother who was supposed to have surgery the next day – only to be told upon arrival that her mother had cancelled the surgery due to some issues that had come up.

Lynn's mother didn't call to let her know before she drove down because she thought it would be nice for her to spend the week anyway. In the meantime, Lynn was getting ready to start a new job and making the trip to help her mother was a necessity, not a luxury, of time and expense – which her mother knew – and especially since her other two sisters had refused to be involved. Without going into all the underlying issues of emotional abuse and abandonment directed at Lynn her whole life, suffice to say that, once again, she felt trapped between the passive abuse and helplessness of her mother and the guilt of not being compassionate enough.

I asked her what she wanted to do, and she said, "I just want to turn around and go back to New York. But I can't because it's late and I'm exhausted from driving all day." And then she had a thought that she would drive an hour north and spend the night with her sister and then drive the rest of the way back in the morning. And she kept saying, "but I still feel so guilty about leaving her, I should have more compassion..." and so on. I suggested that where compassion was most needed in that moment was with herself, and that if she would be willing to have compassion for herself above everyone else, then she would know what to do.

We got off the phone, and she called back a couple hours later for an update. "I decided to leave," she said, "and was on the road to my sister's house when both my sisters called. Everyone suddenly stepped up to help do what was needed so that mom could have the surgery." In that two hours time, all the issues were reconciled and the surgery was back on.

Lynn saw that standing up for her own truth, and having compassion for herself first, made everybody else step up – not only her sisters, which was huge because of all the harbored anger and resentment – but also people outside the family rallied who had caused the crisis of other issues which led to her mother canceling the surgery. And all in only two hours! Interestingly, Lynn's call updating me came just as I was putting the final dot on the "Amen..." in CHAVAKIAH's message of reconciliation!

My story. Some of the hardest healings in our lives involve our parents. We have such a deep need within us to have loving and good parents, that when it all goes wrong we can be affected our whole lives. I am one of those. My journey of healing with my mother began by accepting how I truly felt and finally disowning her as my mother – without feeling guilty about it!

My mother and I had been at odds our whole lives. Still in her teens when I was born, she had never been loved and parented properly herself. But I didn't understand that as a kid – all I saw was that my Mom was still a kid, and not a "safe" parent to rely on or learn from. As the oldest of what would be four of us within a few years, I grew myself up fast and helped with taking care of the younger kids and the house. Mom was eventually married five times in her unending search for the love she so desperately wanted. But I didn't really understand all the husbands coming and going. All I knew was that I was mad at her for divorcing my Dad, and then mad at her for years of abuse of all kinds – some of which she had a heavy hand in – knocking me around whenever I would try to tell her the "truth about things" – especially what she didn't protect us from. And later I was mad at her for my brother's suicide. But before this story makes you cringe too much, let me just interject that I love my Mom, who passed a few years ago, and all of this is told now without the anger and hurt I once had. I learned love and compassion for my mother by finally having enough compassion for myself to walk out of her life.

The breaking point was my trying to tell her years later one last time about the truths in my childhood – something she had never wanted to hear. In this one more attempt I was met by more anger and denial. When she hung up the phone on me, I remember a weight being lifted as I realized that I didn't need her to be my mother anymore – and I felt absolutely no guilt about it. It was one of the most freeing moments of my life.

In the months that followed something remarkable happened. I was in bed reading a book about healing one night when I heard an inner voice tell me to put my fingertips along the scar line I had from a surgery on my abdomen. The area around the scar had become hard and numb evidently from scar tissue. I placed my fingertips there, and then was "told" what was happening in my mother's life when she was pregnant with me – about her finding out that my father was cheating on her – and that all her hurt and anger went right into her belly, where I was residing at the time. And then the voice told me that all the lifelong issues I had carried in my own belly were not mine, but hers visited upon me – and that by my own healing I would help her to heal too.

This had so much resonance for me that I cried until I finally fell asleep. In the morning the hardness in my belly was gone, and the other issues I had in that area my whole life also began to heal over the next few weeks. I felt, as the phrase goes, reborn, and soon I found myself thinking about my mother's disappointment in life, her own pain and how she had never been loved the way she needed to be – in the true and right way we all need to be. By now it was Spring and Easter was coming. I decided to get on a plane and show up at her door to take her for an Easter brunch. I didn't make the connection till later about the symbolism of resurrection – but that's exactly what happened.

When we sat down at lunch, the first thing I did was to thank her for everything she did to keep us together and put food on the table when we were kids – and especially to thank her for divorcing my father. She dropped her fork on that one! For the first time in our lives, we began to talk – really talk. She confirmed the events with my father during her pregnancy with me, and she was able to hear from me everything that had happened during our childhood. We explained ourselves and our lives to each other without holding back anything. It was amazing. The next day I flew back to New York, and a few days later she called me sobbing, apologizing over and over for everything that had ever happened. She had been crying since I left she said. I had already healed in the months before, so I was free to feel so much compassion for her – and to be available now to have a mother and be a daughter for the first time in my life.

My mother and I shared a Birth Angel – her Heart Angel was ARIEL (Perceiver and Revealer), which is my Incarnation Angel. My mother and I enjoyed our new relationship for a few years before she died one morning, uncannily, of a heart attack a couple days before Mother's Day on one of ARIEL's heart days of influence. I knew that this was a message to me about our connection and work together that I might not understand fully until much later. But I know now that at least part of the message is about the power of love and compassion to perceive and reveal the whole truth of us so that we can help each other heal.

Expanding Our Healing Circles

As our lives progress and our circles of relatings widen, we experience both challenging and remarkable encounters with friends, peers, colleagues and even total strangers. Through all of them the thread of healing and helping continues – sometimes as a gossamer filament that ripples lightly between us, and sometimes as a lifeline at the end of our rope.

Friends in need. I will never forget the times in my life when someone just sat with me in my emotional pain – and if

I needed to talk, they listened. I remember three incidents in particular. One was with my friend, Kathy, who as I was crying and pouring out my grief, suddenly burst into tears herself. Suddenly my pain was not just mine, but hers too. I was so surprised that I still had tears running down my face while a surge of release and joy coursed through my body! And then there was the day my close friend, Arnie, who, during the worst relationship breakup of my life when I could not eat or sleep for days, cancelled a studio recording he had booked and showed up at my door with matzo ball soup and orange juice. He sat at the edge of the couch the whole day and fed me, and let me cry, and fed me some more. And then there was Stacy (different friend), with whom I shared years ago a few things about my childhood while we were driving somewhere. She listened quietly as she kept her eyes on the road, and when I turned to look at her there were tears running down her face. These are the miracles of compassion that help us to heal.

My favorite legend in literature is about the Fisher King, King Arthur, the Knights of the Round Table and their quest for the Holy Grail. Briefly, the Holy Grail, which had been in the keeping of the Great King, was lost by a sin he committed, leaving his kingdom a wasteland and himself with a mysterious unhealed wound. After years of searching for the Grail, only three Knights proved worthy of finding it and were able to survive the trials of their quest and finally arrive at the Grail Castle. Of these, Galahad was the one who asked the wounded Fisher King the transformative two-part question of compassion, "Sire, what ails thee...how may I help thee?" Instantly the Grail reappeared, the King was healed and the wasteland of his kingdom restored to vitality.

The "Fisher King" is a translation of the French term, "Le roi pecheur," which means both the Fisher King, as the "fisher of men" (the Christ), and "the sinner king" (Adam). This implies one of the beautiful mysteries at the heart of this legend. We are both Divine and Human. The Knight extended compassion to one who was wounded in his humanity, which restored his true kingship (divinity) and made him and the land whole again as the Grail reappeared. I realize even more through my work with the Angelic Energies that this is a deeply symbolic story about how treating each other with kindness and compassion can restore us to our true and full Divine-Human nature.

I love stories of people helping each other. In fact, I mostly use my Facebook account not as much to report my own doings as to take 10 minutes or so to uplift my day perusing videos and messages depicting mutual kindness between humans, as well as between animals of different species – which of course is a teaching we humans would do well to learn! Around the time I was writing this passage, I saw a video about a man who stopped to help a homeless man check his lottery ticket to see if he won. It turns out he did win – or perhaps the "good Samaritan" staged his win? In any event, the homeless man was told that he won $1000 – which utterly stunned him with surprise and joy. But what really affected him was that when he insisted again and again that the stranger who helped him take some of the money, the helper refused and told him that the money was all his, meant for him and he didn't want anything. The homeless man began to cry and hugged the man for dear life, and said that no one in his whole life had ever done anything for him so caring. He was like the healed Fisher King in that moment –

and just watching that video healed something somewhere in me too.

Healer-helper. My friend Chuck Pisa is an Esoteric Healer. Esoteric Healing works to clean, clear and balance the etheric energy field surrounding our bodies where it is said that all disease and dysfunction starts, and which is sometimes held on the etheric level for years before a physical condition begins to manifest. Through Esoteric Healing, an optimum condition is set for the body to heal, if that is what the soul wants. Having worked with the 72 Angels every morning in meditation for quite some time, with his clients' permissions he began to incorporate their Birth Angels during healing sessions. I asked Chuck to tell me a little about this.

> "I am always amazed and encouraged in my sessions with how much smoother the energy flow is for my clients when invoking their Birth Angels, and how much more the client seems to respond to the session. The presence of the Birth Angels seems to add another dimension to an already multi-dimensional healing. Since the daily Angel wisdoms have been available, I now also incorporate the particular Angel for the day along with the client's Incarnation Angel. It never ceases to amaze me how uncanny the synchronicity is between that day's Angel wisdom, the client's Birth Angel and what is going on in his or her life. Sometimes it helps me (or should I say "they" help me) to zero-in on a particular pattern that may need to be attended to by my client. All in all, I certainly welcome the help and my clients appreciate it as well, so that we both can continue in our healing "joy-ney."

A few months ago, Chuck's healing work dove-tailed with Stacie when she was visiting from out of town before a scheduled surgery for a condition that had strangely developed and was getting worse over the months. It was now, to spare some details, abscessed and she was very uncomfortable. I suggested to her that she see Chuck for a session while she was here, and she did so. Some emotional things came up in the session which precipitated a release, and that night the abscess drained and she felt a palpable healing. Since she was working regularly with the 72 Angels, we thought to check the Angel for that day, which was MITZRAEL for Internal Reparation! The next week she asked the doctor to check her out before the surgery in case she didn't need it. He did so, and told her that amazingly the abscess had healed, but there was still a tiny hole that he needed to sew up. The surgery happened to be done on the Angel day of HARIEL, for Purification!

The first Angelic correspondence in her story is pretty uncanny too. Rewind to her frustrating odyssey with various doctors trying to find out what her condition was, when one morning she awoke with a knowing that this was the day she was going to find a doctor who would be able to figure out what she had and what to do about it. By 10 o'clock, her previous doctor had called to tell her she made an appointment for her with a specialist to see that morning. By noon the new doctor had figured out exactly what she had and how to treat it. When she called me after her doctor's visit, we realized that the Heart Angel of the day was ARIEL, as Perceiver and Revealer (again, my own Incarnation Angel).

Mining the Good from the "Bad"

In this volume, the Angel MANAKEL, representing the Knowledge of Good and Evil, delivered the longest message – some four pages! And it's no wonder since this subject is so central to how we define our relatings with each other and everything that happens in our world. Since MANAKEL has so much to say about this, I'll leave it for the Wisdom (#66).

Interestingly, Stacie's Heart Angel is MANAKEL, which has inspired conversation between us about the nature of "bad" – especially when good comes out of it. She recounted to me two instances of seemingly bad things that happened to her which turned out to be life-altering experiences – one that brought love into her life and the other which saved her life.

"When I was 16, I was T-boned by another car after running a stop sign that I didn't see. At the time, I labeled it as a 'bad' experience. However, because of the wreck, I had to drive down to Cabot, a small town where I grew up before moving to Little Rock, to purchase a replacement door. While there, I dropped by my childhood friend's home, and she invited me to go to the lake. There I met the first love of my life, Chris. Had it not been for the car wreck, I wouldn't have met Chris and had that incredible first-love experience. That car wreck introduced me to a new kind of love, different from family and friends, and gave me the awareness I would need many times in my life to look beyond a singular event and not attach a 'good' or 'bad' connotation to it.

Years later, I had another life-altering experience in a whole different way. A carload of men pulled up beside me as if to pass on a curvy road, but instead rammed into my driver's side of the car. It was dark, and I lost control of my car, then regained control and ended up stalled and facing the opposite direction I was heading in. They pulled up to my window and the driver pointed a gun at me, yelling for me to get out of the car. In that moment, my consciousness seemed to pop out of my body, and I was able to dispassionately view the situation from another perspective. It was as if time stopped, and in what must have been only a few seconds I was able to 'see' that my car was still running and that I could act faster than they could react. So I floored it, and my car took off in the opposite direction they were facing. Thankfully I wasn't hurt, and I later realized that something I considered as 'evil' for a very long time was actually an opportunity in my life to experience my consciousness alter and observe the situation from a different psychological reality. Without the emotional fuel of intense fear, I don't know if I would have had that 'super-reality' kind of experience, and consequently, experiential 'proof' that our consciousness is something that is mobile."

Occasionally I have been struck by a remarkable story of someone in the news who was able to stop a crime and thwart harm to themselves and others by showing compassion to a perpetrator. I remember two such stories in the last year, one case involving the invasion of a school and the other of a private home, both by an armed intruder. In each circumstance, it was the kindness and compassion a woman showed to the gunman that got him to finally surrender without harming anyone.

I experienced something similar on a New York City street many years ago with a deli delivery boy. The firm I was working for at the time had complained to the deli about his behavior and the state of the food when he delivered lunch to us, and so I had to take the food back and pick up a new order. When I got there, the boy was in the process of being fired, which he decided to take out on me. While I was waiting for the food, he evidently got a knife and went outside to wait for me to come out. One of the customers saw him and told the manager. The manager sent the cook (who was a big guy) out with me when I was ready to leave. The boy lunged at me, and the cook stopped him and we began yelling at each other. Suddenly something in me shifted. As I looked at him and saw his pain, I felt a presence come between us, and time seemed to stop as everyone around us faded into the background. I began to cry and took his hand and said, "look at how we are treating each other....I am so sorry for my part in all this." He was so shocked that he began to cry too, and he dropped the knife. We embraced, both knowing that something extraordinary was happening.

Several months later I was walking down the street in a different part of town, and I heard someone call out to me. There he was selling vegetables at a corner stand – and he was beaming at me with the smile of a saint! I stopped to talk to him and we hugged, and I felt so incredibly blessed to see how he was. And though I never saw him again, I have never forgotten him and the gifts we were both given in our transformative encounter together.

TERAH COX

Daily Life with the 72 Angels

As I continue with the Daily Wisdoms, I continue to be "amazed but not surprised" at the uncanny synchronicities, increasing spiritual "life-support" and cultivation of awareness in people's lives through their daily communions with the Angels. From the feedback I receive from readers, it seems the Wisdoms have become a daily touchstone for many. Some read them in the morning as a kind of "pre-set button" to set their awareness for the day to pay attention and work purposefully on the qualities of that day's Heart Angel, and some in the evening to review the day's events from the prevailing "angle" of Divine light that day.

I really enjoy the ending and beginning days that bridge one Angel cycle with another because every time there is a lot of movement and change in people's lives, including my own. During the end days of writing this volume, there seemed to be a rash of people who were experiencing chaotic endings, changes and new events on the days leading up to the end of the last Angel cycle and the beginning of this one – especially the 72nd Angel MUMIAH, for Endings and Rebirth, and the first Angel VEHUIAH for Will and New Beginnings. My goddaughter, Lindy, wrote me, "I was having a really off-day the other day, and then the next morning I saw that the wisdom was about new beginnings and it helped me to reset." A friend told me her father broke up with his girlfriend on MUMIAH's day, and she traveled a few hours to visit him the next day (VEHUIAH) to help him "start fresh" by putting his house in order for winter. Another friend started a new job on VEHUIAH's day, and several people started working with new clients in the first week of the new cycle, many of whom seemed to be going through their own endings and beginnings.

Ongoing Work and Play with the Angels

The 72 Angels Daily Wisdoms help to increase awareness and utilization of our magnificent inner resources – the soul-voice within our hearts and our Angelic support system designed to amplify the Divine within all the inner and outer parts of our human beingness. Thus we might become the true and fulfilled Divine-Human beings we are here to be. As we begin to experience the Angels in this light, we see this greater potential of ourselves, each other and all of life. There is so much more to see than we are looking at, so much more to feel than we are reaching for, so much more to know than what has been handed down to us by others.

As we allow the Angels to take up more of our inner room, there is less space for doubts, fears, guilt, shame and old hurts, and more room for the truth of who we are and the self-love that enables us to truly love others. Looking through our "Angel-eyes," we see their messages and gifts waiting in the wings of every moment, encounter, conversation and coincidence. Our daily lives become full of signs, wonders, symbols and clues to unlock the meanings and purposes of our gifts, opportunities and challenges.

Through the Angels we come to understand that we each exist as a uniqueness of being and potential within the Divine Oneness, and the Divine Oneness exists within us in order to enhance the qualities and powers of our humanity – while at the same time enabling the Divine to experience life as only each of us can live it. Thus, when we welcome the Angels as *angles*, or qualities, of Divine Light – we are not asking them to come to us from "Above." What we are actually doing is inviting our awareness to see that they are already here within and around and among us. By welcoming them, we acknowledge their presence and our willingness to engage their Divine magnificence shimmering within us as the potential of our own magnificence.

And so, as in the Divine-Human mysteries of many spiritual paths and vocabularies, we are called to three things in our work and play with the Angels: **ask**, **receive** and **become**. This ongoing 3-step "Angel-alchemy" can ultimately transform our base *mettle* into the spiritual gold of a being who is fulfilled in the wholeness and co-creation of love and truth. Remember as you do this that you are working with specific aspects and energies of the Divine Itself, as "angles" of the Divine Light that It is – not separate created beings:

1. **Ask** (Invoke) – Pray/chant/speak the Angel's name, open your heart and invite its presence to expand within you.

2. **Receive** (Imbibe) – Breathe in, listen, meditate upon and allow the Angel's essence and energy to expand within your heart and being.

3. **Become** (Embody) – Absorb, digest and assimilate the Angel's qualities into the very belly of your beingness so that your awareness and your action come into harmony (as in 'walking the talk').

These steps can be part of a meditation with the day's Angel and used to focus attention and awareness for everything you encounter during your day. Most importantly, follow the inner prompts from that not so still, not so small voice in your heart, for it may be the voice of the Angel within, in unison with and amplification of your own soul and its purposes. Slowly, or even epiphanously, the effects become cumulative and life-transforming.

I suggest to create some quiet time for a few moments every day to read and contemplate the day's Angel-wisdom. Remember that the message is meant to speak to your heart, and note the parts that resonate with you. As you go through your day notice what is echoed in conversations and encounters, and where you can use the qualities of that day's Angel to be more heartful with yourself, your work and others. Pay attention to the moments that trigger a feeling, which will indicate a timely relevance to you. Begin to see the connections between you and everything and everyone which are sometimes signaled by coincidence and unexpected encounters. And for every question you have and whatever truth you seek, consider that the answer is love – and look to what love is calling you to in that moment.

The Seasons of Our Lives

The Angels tell us that this plane of existence is NOT an illusion. What is an illusion is to think that this world's reality, or our own outer beingness, is *all* there is. Sometimes we are like leaves so far out on our branches that we forget the source that supports us, the roots that sustain us, and the heart-sap that nourishes us. We're just out there waving in the wind, soaking in the light. Nevertheless, for all our own forgetting, we are not forgotten by the source itself as we continue to be sustained for all our days. And then the day comes when like the leaf, our forms fall and what we leave behind becomes nutrients for those who come after us. No longer contained and constricted in form, our essence is freed to experience that, however magnificent it was to be a leaf or a physical being, we are now, and once again, far more than we were as physical forms. For our greater life – our essential life – is eternal. The greatest opportunity of our humanity is to remember and experience this while we are still physical beings so that our experience of living might be magical!

We can learn so much from nature about being both form and essence. Thus, the Angels' Daily Wisdoms follow the flow and energies of the seasons expressed in the natural world and also in our own lives. Just as with the Divine and the entire cosmos since the first "moments" of Emanation and differentiation of the One into the many of Creation, everything and everyone is birthed and moves through life not only seasonally, but daily, through cycles of ebb and flow in the context of **relationship**. The 72 Angels yearly cycle begins March 21, with our relationship with the Divine and our soul's cosmic birth, from which all else emerges. The 72 Angels in their daily heart dominion cycle five times a year (72 x 5 + some overlapping days = 365):

Spring ~ 3/21–6/2: Relationship with the Divine. The newborn green of Spring symbolizes our cosmic birth and what the soul regards as our primary relationship with the Divine Itself as our origin. Just as with the Spring rebirth of many forms of Creation in the natural world, we too experience the quickening and joy of new being as we begin to sprout new beginnings and creations that have been gestating within us during the Winter.

Summer ~ 6/3–8/16: Relationship with self. This is a time of exploration and celebration of ourselves through self-love, compassion, forgiveness, gladness, a lighterness of being and the flowering and ripening of our unique potentials.

Fall ~ 8/17–10/29: <u>Relationship with work and purpose.</u> This is the season for harvesting the fruits of our summer and scattering new seeds as we get back to work after vacations and times of fun and relaxation with family and friends. While outer forms begin to fall away, we begin a deeper exploration into meaning and purpose as we continue to cultivate our individuation through new ideas and projects.

The "Holy-days" of Late Fall/Early Winter ~ 10/30–1/8: <u>Relationship with others.</u> Here the Angels bring us to heart-and-mindfulness in our interpersonal relatings at the time of year when we gather with loved ones and those in our immediate circles to celebrate the holidays and holy days of the season. In coming together with those who matter most, where the need for healing is often most apparent, we see the opportunity through self-transformation to transform our relationships.

Winter ~ 1/9–3/20: <u>Relationship with community and the world.</u> The Angel wisdoms here bring the five Angelic cycles to completion in focusing on how we contribute our individuation, purposes and interpersonal relatings to our communities and the consciousness of humankind. In the seeming dormancy of winter, we cultivate more of who we are and what we bring to the world by infusing greater depth and purpose into our endeavors. Through the gestation and nurturing of new ideas, new wisdoms soon begin to sprout for a refreshed and even reborn self in the Spring.

As previously mentioned, the seasonal references in the Angel wisdoms would be reversed for those in the southern hemisphere, with the seasons being less dramatic for those who live closer to the equator.

Nurturing the Seeds of the Holi-Days

From October through the beginning of January is the time of year when much of the world is gathering with family and friends to commemorate the holidays and holy days in our different rituals of family, culture and creed. There is much emphasis on the where and how of gatherings – and for those who are not as religiously observant, the emphasis is often on family dynamics, communal meals and gift-giving.

However differently the holidays and holy days are celebrated, there seems to be a similar thread that runs through the whole season for most everyone – and that is the *spirit* of the season. This is when love, kindness, compassion, generosity and forgiveness are especially "in the air" to be given and shared – and it is also the time when we feel the pain and regret for both the past and the present when these seem to be missing. **But there is no more potent time for healing and the rebirth of togetherness precisely because the spirit of love, which can heal anything, is heightened all around us and within us.**

Many people have tired of the rituals of the holidays, some because of difficult family dynamics, some because of over-commercialism and unreasonable or disappointed expectations – and some who feel that we should be gifting each other all year long with things and ways of being that are often reserved only for the holidays, which they feel makes our holiday gatherings and gifts seem contrived. My own feeling about the holidays is that, as our one "day of rest" is meant to be in our week, we preserve certain rituals and traditions to have some being time in all our doing – to relax our striving and remember what and who matter most that give meaning and purpose to all we do. For those who want to exercise spiritual connection, holy days are also an opportunity to "be still and know that I am," with the Divine that powers our humanity.

Gift-giving teaches us to both give and receive, but it means different things to different people. For some, gifting is a reflection of love, connection and appreciation, with consideration of what would be meaningful or enjoyable to the recipient. For others, the gift is a substitute for the greater inner gift that may be harder to give. The greatest gift of the season for everyone, however, is the only gift that costs nothing but our willingness and keeps on giving – and that is the gift of love.

In this time of year when the qualities and dynamics of our relationships are even moreso, we have such powerful resources within our hearts to expand and express our love – whether that means unearthing it from behind layers of harbored hurts and old angers, resentments and disappointments – or magnifying the love that is readily here between and among us. These resources – gifts which the Angels tell us are forged in the grace of the Divine-Human heart – are compassion, understanding and forgiveness.

When we leap over the walls of our various religious dogmas, we see that in the mystical hearts of all traditions flow these gifts of the heart. Particularly in Christianity, this season symbolizes the birth of love, compassion and forgiveness in the human physicality of Jesus the Christ as "the Word become flesh" – one who was a gift given by the Divine Heart unto humanity to show us how to love and forgive ourselves and each other – and that the "Way" to the "Father," each other and our own transformation is through love. The heart-centered teachings of Jesus show us that when we are willing to set aside our diverse personal and religious dogmas, attitudes, issues and old hurts which keep us divided – and simply meet in our sameness of heart – we can see ourselves and the other through the love-light of the "kingdom of Heaven" within us and be transformed. As 72 "angles" of this very love-light dwelling within us, the Angels convey to us the same message and meaning.

Because angels are especially prevalent in the Judaic and Christic histories as messengers and guardians, this is also a time of year when angels are in the mass consciousness (and also of course highly commercialized). On a deeper level, however, the 72 Angels tradition illuminates the roles of the angels far beyond their popular forms and meanings. As conveyors of the Divine Heart into our own, they are the multiplied presences of the Divine Being dwelling within us to amplify and ennoble the capacities of our humanity. And so, particularly in this season of inner and outer lights – which includes Judaism's "Festival of Lights" during Hanukkah – the wisdom messages of the 72 Angels are all about the awakening of love, healing, transformation and renewal between and among us, so that we might see each other's light and "absolutely sparkle together."

TERAH COX

The Daily Wisdoms

The 72 Angels' Days of Heart Influence

In case you did not start the *Book of Days* series with the first three volumes, repeated here with a few revisions are the various associations accompanying the Daily Angel Wisdoms which relate to the Angel's position on the Tree of Life, and also give clues to its nature: the Sephira of the Tree in which the Angel resides, its overlighting Archangel, astrological and date correspondences and more.

Introductory Pages: These introduce the Sephira (vessel or sphere) in which each group (choir) of eight Angels reside on the Tree of Life, as well as the qualities and functions of the overlighting Archangel.

Date: The current day of the Angel's expression through our heart plane is bolded; the other dates represent its four other "heart-days" of influence and support during the year. Since it is helpful to be aware of your Heart Angel not only on your birthday, but also its other four days of influence, you may want to mark your personal calendar with all five days. Note also that the yearly cycle for the 72 Angels begins March 21, the time of the Spring Equinox, which is the beginning of "Nissan," the first month of the year in the Jewish calendar. In my research I also ran across an obscure variant in the date attributions of the Angelic cycles, but the one used in all the *Birth Angels* materials is the cycle that the 12th-15th century school of Isaac the Blind and his followers were working with and which is most used throughout the centuries. (See Appendix II)

An Angel's full day of influence goes from 12:00 am midnight to 12:00 am midnight, 24 hours later (00:00-24:00 in Europe, etc.). A few of the Angels' days overlap to support a total of 365 days. In a leap year of 366 days, the Angel for February 28 also governs the 29th. The "am" designation always goes from 12:00 am midnight to 12:00 pm noon (00:00-12), and the "pm" from 12:00 pm noon to 12:00 am midnight (12:00-24:00). Of course, 12:00 is a cusp minute for both day and night. An Angel that governs for a day and a half, for example, 4/16 + 17 am, would span from 12:00 am midnight as the 15th passes to the 16th to 12:00 pm on the 17th (midnight to midnight to noon) (00:00-24:00-12:00).

Angel's number and name: The number for each Angel represents the order of its position on the Tree of Life and its degrees of correspondence to the Zodiacal wheel of time – and if you study astrology and numerology these may give additional insight into both the Angels and the stars. The Angel's name is a transliteration of its Hebrew name. The origin of the names is from what the Kabbalah refers to as the 72 "Intelligences" or "Names of God" as the "Shem HaMephorash,"), which are each composed of a three-letter combination derived from a "decoding" of Exodus 14:19-21 in Hebrew. While vowels were originally left out of the Angels' Hebrew Names to create ambiguity in order to protect the sacred Names of God, in later centuries the "niqqud" (vowel marks) were added to help with pronunciation. Each Angel's name ends in either "IAH" or "EL," denoting that the name is a Name and Quality of God. Some Kabbalists say that IAH represents the feminine aspect and EL the masculine, representing the inherent masculine-feminine unity within the Divine which is expressed as polarities within all manifestations of life (starting with, scientists long-believed, a positive proton and negative electron – through there has been increasing study of what is called "the God particle,") You will notice if you consult other sources through the ages that the spellings of the Angels' names vary greatly. This is the result of dialects and permutations in the Hebrew language and its transliterations through centuries of dispersion of the Jewish people into different cultures and sects. I have done extensive research on this, but in the end have chosen to follow most of the spellings that the works of Haziel put forth based on the 12th-15th century manuscripts found in the 1975 excavation. (See Volume 1 or Appendix II herein for details.)

Pronunciation guide: This is given to help with saying or chanting the Angel's name aloud in meditation or prayer as you invite the Angel's energies to expand within you. All the names are accented (shown in ALL CAPS) on the last syllable, IAH or EL, to emphasize that the name is a quality and aspect of God. Names with more than two syllables have two accented syllables.

Angel's quality/function and G/R/S designation: This represents the Divine attribute which the Angel embodies and amplifies within you, and whether the attribute is expressed outwardly (G, for "Going out" from the Divine and down the Tree of Life toward manifestation), inwardly (R for "Returning" back up the Tree to the Divine through ascending consciousness), or in a state of equilibrium which can be expressed outwardly or inwardly (S for Stabilized).

Keynote phrase: This is a short by-line I have added to capture the essence of the Angel's function.

Overlighting Archangel: This is the Archangel that governs the Sephira which the Angel resides within on the Tree of Life, and whose qualities overlight or influence the functions of the Angels in that Sephira and the Angelic order (choir) that the Angels belong to. There are eight Angels in each of the Nine (out of Ten) Sephirot on the Tree (8x9=72). It is perhaps worthwhile to note that throughout the world's Angelic traditions, Archangels' roles regarding Earth and humankind are as the guardians of lands, nations and societal groups; whereas the Angels are attendant to individuals because their vibrations are said to be nearer to life forms. However, until this tradition was revealed in 1975, only a few of the Angels' individual names have been commonly known.

The Angel's sign, planet and 5-day period of "Incarnation" influence: The Angel's astrological correspondences relate to its five consecutive days of influence once a year on the Incarnation, or physical, plane, which also corresponds to 5 degrees of the Zodiac (72x5=360). If you are interested in astrology, this can help to shed additional light on the Angel's qualities. (Neptune and Uranus were added later when they were discovered.) Although the Angels in their Incarnation influence (physicality, will and life purpose) are not the focus of this work, I added the dates of each Angel's Incarnation influence (the date spread next to the sign/planet) for ease in discovering your Incarnation Angel – which would be the one governing the five-day span that corresponds to the five-days around your birth. For example, if your birthday is March 18, your Incarnation Angel would be #72 MUMIAH, which governs March 16-20. (See also Appendix I for a complete list of the 72 Angels with their corresponding 5-day span of Incarnation influence.)

"I AM THAT WHICH…:" Here the Angel introduces itself as a particularized aspect ("that which") of the One "I AM" which is its purpose to amplify in our human lives – thus helping us to fulfill the unique "I Am That Which" that each of us are as a particular constellation of Divine-Human qualities.

The Angel's message: As detailed above, all 72 Angels cycle for at least one day five times a year, effectively taking us through the seasons of the year and of our lives. Since everything and everyone exists in the context of relationship, the first cycle of 72 messages starting March 21 start with our soul relationship to the Divine, and in subsequent cycles throughout the year move into our relationship with self, our work and purposes, others in our immediate circles, and then to our communities and the world at large. Thus, all five cycles comprise a journey in one year through all the literal and symbolic themes and seasons of our lives.

In addition, you will likely notice that the Angels have different tones – some are lighter, some more serious, some "teacherly" and others passionate. Also, sometimes an Angel speaks as "I" and sometimes as "we." I continue to sense that in their roles as differentiated expressions of the Divine Oneness, "I" and "we" are interchangeable for them. The light-thread that is woven through all the different messages is love and its power to reveal and expand the truth of who we are and what we are here to be and do with ourselves and each other.

The "Amen" at the end of each Wisdom. I realized I had been hearing "Amen" at the end of each Wisdom from the beginning of the project and had not been fully conscious of it until working on the third volume! "Amen" is a word of power in Hebrew, a kind of cosmic "abracadabra" to activate the Divine in human life. In researching the word's origins, there were the usual Hebrew and Christian uses of Amen as "so be it" at the end of prayers, as well as other correspondences:

Amen encompasses the Hebrew letters "aleph-mem-nun" (confirmed, reliable, have faith, believe), which also corresponds to the word "emuna" (faith) and "emet" (truth). There are also presumed associations with the Egyptian god Amun (also Amen, the creator of all things, king of the gods) and the Hindu Sanskrit word Aum (or Om, the Absolute, Omnipresent, Manifest and Unmanifest). In suddenly becoming fully aware of the "Amen" that was naturally emerging at the end of each wisdom, I realized that the intent of the Angelic Energy was that the words would not only inspire but transmit the energies of their meaning unto those "who have the heart to hear." In the cacophony of life and its demands, we may have the heart to hear in one moment and not in another – so the word Amen is a word to call us back to our hearts from wherever else we are. And so here, as "Amen..." the three dots are meant to extend a loving and compassionate space to do that.

Remember, again, that the Daily Wisdoms are given as messages from the 72 Angels when they are in their "heart dominion," to amplify qualities of Divine Love to support our cultivation of self-love and love of others, as well compassion, understanding, forgiveness, intuition, soul-truth and wisdom. As the Angel JELIEL conveys in Volume 1, "*the Love we bring is a Love composed of as many different qualities, forms, faces and expressions as there are people...a Love that contains all purposes and possibilities...a Love that will be your anchor against time's fickle winds of change and the sometimes stormy seas of life. A Love-light of Truth by which you may see finally that however long or far you seek, what you are looking for is always right here in your heart of hearts, prompting you to ask, beckoning you to receive, inviting you to shine forth more and more of who you truly are. And to know once and for all that, truly, you are not alone – for there is always someone at home...within."*

And so now, may you continue your daily heart-journey with the 72 Angels, the joy of the season's bounty and the nurturing of new seeds in your heart, mind, body and soul!

October 30 – November 6

Angels 1 – 8

Sephira 1

KETHER ~ Crown/Will

Overlighting Archangel

METATRON ~ "Angel of the Presence"
Enlightenment, the connection of Light between
God's energy and human spiritual energy
(Related to the prophet Enoch & Akashic Records)

---

1 **VEHUIAH**
2 **JELIEL**
3 **SITAEL**
4 **ELEMIAH**
5 **MAHASIAH**
6 **LELAHEL**
7 **ACHAIAH**
8 **CAHETEL**

3/21 * 6/3 * 8/17 * **10/30** * 1/9

1 VEHUIAH

(vay-HOO-ee-YAH)
Will and New Beginnings (G)
'One who begins again and again'
Archangel ~ METATRON
Aries / Uranus (3/21-25)

I AM THAT WHICH...

fosters your willingness to begin or renew relationships by starting from the present moment with new perspectives, optimism and vitality, and the ability to distinguish between what is and what could be. The beginnings of relationships are often magical – but that glow or 'love at first sight' may just be you falling in love with your own new self in the other person's eyes! You don't know each other at first, but you do come with all your long-held desires, wishes and dreams about relationship that can easily be projected onto an almost total stranger! A new relationship or friendship must start with what is, not what was or what if, what could be or should be. That means to approach as who you are, and appreciate who the other is in this present moment. Do not enter into personal or intimate relationships thinking about how you can make the other better or help them to be who they really are – or hoping they will complete you so that you can finally be who you truly are. Fall in love with potential if you are a teacher, parent, therapist, employer or mentor! In the meantime, pursue friends and partners who are already your peers.

Everyone has potential, and the truth is, with love everyone's potential is greater, even unlimited. But respect and care for each other as who you are now – then potential will blossom on its own without your pulling at it. All that said, the great thing about beginnings is that you get to start again and be the person you want to be right now! Imagine if you allow your loved ones to do that – to become a new person in your eyes and heart! And yes, there are likely some people in your life with whom it's easier to be your own ever-evolving self. But over time, you can renew long-time relationships through changes in perspective, attitude or interaction. Even with family and friends who always see you and each other as you were so many years ago, the repetition of a changed behavior will eventually make its mark in willing hearts. For the heart is made for new beginnings. No matter what hurts have been harbored, in the face of true caring, compassion and understanding the heart reawakens and welcomes new relationship.

So dear ever-beginning one, let my VEHUIAH light within you be as the light of every day's new dawn, reminding you that today is always a new day, ever emerging from the seeds of yesterday's endings. And know that with the fires of initiative, you and all your relatings can become new in any way you so desire through willingness and trust in the power of the heart to be reborn again and again. Amen...

3/22 * 6/4 * 8/18 + 19am * **10/31** * 1/10

2 JELIEL

(YAY-lee-EL)
Love and Wisdom (G)
'One who uses love to make wisdom'
Archangel ~ METATRON
Aries / Saturn (3/26-30)

I AM THAT WHICH...

helps to deepen and transport your relationships to new heights with the values, wisdoms and creation energies of love. Love is not only about feelings. Love is the 'prime-mover' of your evolving truths, your powers as a human being and the light in all your relatings. Feelings are the compelling compass, and sparkle, in the wonder of love. By love's guidance system of feeling, you are drawn to romantic partners, friendships, creativities and endeavors that are most true for you. And though it is the feeling of love that makes you cherish and seek it out – it is love's multifaceted nature that makes it so valuable and necessary to the fullness of your life and your relationships.

The values of love are seeded by compassion and forgiveness of self and others. From these are harvested kindness, mercy, wisdom and well-being at the expense of no one, including the Earth itself. Without love, anything or anyone may be broken and infringed against. And when brokenness occurs between you, only love can make you whole again. Because love is the author of wholeness, it is love's nature to be inclusive in order to show you the *underlying unity that connects you to each other – even while you express the diversity of the Divine Itself through your own diverse beings, paths and ways.*

It is the wisdom of love which transforms any knowledge or experience you bring to it into a greater knowing and seeing. For anything you may think you know about another, love's wisdom fills out the rest of the story with a more whole truth. For love sees not only what is visible, but what is still evolving in the unseen realms of heart and soul. Thus love's wisdom within you sees not only who others are, but who they long to become. And love's understanding knows that there is an essential goodness in each and all.

Finally and ongoingly, love is the alpha and the omega of existence and all that is possible between and among beings. For love is God's creation energy, the verb of all that is Divine (and there's nothing that is not!) and the prime and quantum mover of creation, matter and the truths of all souls, beings, bodies, minds and hearts – that even when seemingly immoveable long to soar. It is only with the powers of love that anything or anyone can begin, and transform all endings into new beginnings again. Only with love may your relatings be renewed and restored. Only with love may the truth of a being, a relationship, a community or world be fully revealed and expanded, even into a new truth.

Thus my JELIEL light is given within you so you may see that your soul and the souls of all others, without exception, were conceived and made in and of love. And thus, it is love you must return to in order to fulfill the truth of yourselves in relationship with each other. And we wish you to know this mystery about your relatings: The only truly transformative power that you possess to change another is *love – but the change will be what is true and right for them. When you extend love to another through the <u>feelings</u> or <u>actions</u> of acceptance, compassion and forgiveness, you surround them with love's creation energy and the power to tap it if they so desire. Once love's presence has been amplified by your grace in giving it, love is like water – taking the shape of whatever it fills, and filling the invisible and seemingly impenetrable spaces where love has been forgotten. As love seeps down into the roots of a person to bring nourishment and life, you may not see the fruit until their own season of ripening is at hand. Thus dear one, while you may sometimes see yourself and others 'through a glass darkly' in your individual life seasons, know that it is always love you are looking at. Amen...*

TERAH COX

3/23 * 6/5 * 8/19pm + 20 * **11/1** * 1/11

3 SITAEL

(SIT-ah-EL)
Construction of Worlds (G)
'One who loves creations into being'
Archangel ~ METATRON
Aries / Jupiter (3/31-4/4)

I AM THAT WHICH...

helps to create a harmonious personal world of 'house and home' as a place of mutual love, comfort and support and the foundation of values for everything you build in your relatings together. The foundational structure that deeply affects all your ongoing relationships is the home you experienced with the first inhabitants of your heart. This is usually your family, early friendships and 'first loves.' Perhaps those cornerstones were strong, supportive and good, and you carry them forward as such. Or, if disruption and difficulty occurred, it may be that your future cornerstones have become stronger because of that early 'cracked foundation,' weak 'support beams' and ruptures of heart and home that resulted. Or maybe some of your cornerstones still encase some of the the brokenness of the past. This is when you may call upon the strength of your Divine home, your home of soul-origin, to heal the wounds of that first earthly home, so that you may model your present and future relatings not on that broken structure – but on the home of your soul and the greater knowing it conveys to your heart about what is true, loving and right.

For this remodeling to occur, your soul may ask your secretly hurting heart to feel compassion for the brokenness and corruption of your first earthly home. In the light of compassion, you can more easily see that those who may have broken your heart did so from the brokenness of their own. The hurts done to you did not start with them, but with the hurts of their forefathers upon them. If you can forgive them, then it is you who will stop the hemorrhage of the past into the present, and you who will become the healer of your family, and the generations, at long last. And then you will be free finally to create a new home in your world with stronger and more loving cornerstones that reflect the values of your own heart, your own love and wisdom, your own greater understanding.

And for all this you are given my SITAEL light to see and know that you may always rebuild your world and your relationships with the cornerstones of willingness, love, compassion and forgiveness. For these are infinitely greater than any one memory, any one hurt, any legacy of pain and divisiveness. Love, as Divine creation energy, is a builder and a rebuilder, and no force can truly or permanently tear asunder what love has built, though the forms of love may come and go. And thus, may you go forth with love to rebuild any relationships which may be cracked, weakened and 'sagging,' trusting in love as your architect, your building blocks and the soft and fluid mortar that holds your world together and gives your heart a place to come home to within each other. Amen...

3/24 * 6/6 * 8/21 * **11/2** * 1/12

4 ELEMIAH

(eh-LEM-ee-YAH)
Divine Power (G)
'One who implants the tree of life within'
Archangel ~ METATRON
Aries / Mars (4/5-9)

I AM THAT WHICH...

helps you to heal power struggles with loved ones, friends and colleagues by realizing that the only true and abiding power is the power of love, which empowers all and yet claims sovereignty over none. What is thought of as power in relatings and relationships is measured in many different ways. You may speak of being 'over-powered' or having power over, being empowered or disempowered, being in power, taking or wielding power or giving or not giving your power away. Perceptions of power are often mistaken for issues of control, money, position, prestige and so on. But true power cannot be acquired, stolen, bartered, bought or relinquished. True power is an existential birthright which the Spirit endows unto each soul as a particular likeness of Itself to be cultivated within the human heart and held in balance by higher mind. True power is about tapping into the creation energy of love which composes the essence of who you are, and which powers your biological, mental and emotional processes at the most minute levels. True power has a sense of the origin and miracle of life and strives to exercise respect, wisdom and care for self and others.

This does not mean that there are not hierarchies of authority within a family or organization. But those who hold positions of authority have the most responsibility to practice the right use of power. When children are respected, they learn to respect themselves and tap into their own inner power to explore their interests, potentials and who they want to become. When elders are honored, they are empowered with a sense of dignity and worthwhileness. When students are engaged enthusiastically, they feel empowered to learn. When employees are valued, they are committed and caring about their work.

With partners and friendships, and any relating that involves peers, mutual respect and sharing of power (as the energies of love) must be integral to the relationship. With true caring, the innate power of each is acknowledged, even guarded by the other, and you take comfort in relying on each other without taking the other for granted. There is recognition and appreciation for your individualities and the unique ways in which each of you contribute to the whole that is the relationship. And if the relationship is threatened, returning to love and respect will empower truth to be offered, received and evolved.

My ELEMIAH light of Divine Power is in the very cell-and-soul-structure of your Divine-Human beingness, and I invite you to call upon this light that is within you whenever your power is abused or misused by yourself or another. But know that it cannot be taken from you. Always return to the heart-force within and the love that you are, that you may remember and reclaim the power that is uniquely yours, which has never left you and never will. Amen...

3/25 * 6/7 * 8/22 * **11/3** * 1/13

5 MAHASIAH

(ma-HA-see-YAH)
Rectification (G)
'One who returns to what is true for love's sake'
Archangel ~ METATRON
Aries / Sun (4/10-14)

I AM THAT WHICH...

illuminates difficulties in interpersonal dynamics, even if originated generations earlier, in order to right 'wrongs' which continue to cause disruption and dysfunction. Often it can take a lifetime or even generations for a hurt or wrongdoing to be corrected and healed. This is because the chain of reactions from that original wrong is visited upon one person to another and another until it becomes integrated into ancestral legacies. However, all it takes is one person to stop reacting to the accumulated pain and dysfunction – one who will make a choice that is no longer reactionary, so that the chain of cause and effect can be broken and the past can begin to be healed and rectified. This independent act of love and willingness first involves acceptance and forgiveness of self – which enables these to then be extended to the others. **Forgiveness is for giving your life back to yourself –** *for it is only then when you may lay down the burden of the past and embrace the present. It is the choice to exercise love in the present that changes the past by changing its effect on you. This is the work of a compassionate heart following the higher calling of the soul to become free.*

Every time you do harm to yourself or another, you indenture yourself to the natural laws that always seek the restoration of balance. A harbored sense of guilt without restorative action paralyzes true atonement. Guilt is meant not to shame or hold you hostage, but to instantly let you know when you have caused hurt to another. If your reaction is to strive to ease that hurt instead of wallowing in self-judgment, then you will be able to liberate yourself and those around you from ongoing hurt. Love does not mean 'never having to say you're sorry,' but being willing to do so – and then set about mending the fragmentation of self from which offenses to self and others are caused.

Love and truth are the great healers, and through them all things can be rectified. That does not mean there won't be consequences. But with the love-and-truth energies that are the compositional aspects of the Divine Itself, which is also your own, those consequences will be experienced less as a punishment than an opportunity for purification and course-correction. Finally, with love you come home to the foundational and untarnished truth of the essential goodness and purpose of your being.

So my MAHASIAH light of rectification within you asks you only this: are you willing to be healed and allow your true course to be illuminated and set before you? If so, then I invite you to become 'yes-hearted' without concern about the details of how it will be done. Know only that it will come as love, in one form or another, looking for the love within you. Amen...

3/26 * 6/8 * 8/23 * **11/4** * 1/14

6 LELAHEL

(LAY-la-HEL)
Light of Understanding (G)
'One who transforms knowledge'
Archangel ~ METATRON
Aries / Venus (4/15-20)

I AM THAT WHICH...

helps to increase within your heart the light of understanding, which gives you an external glow of loving-kindness that attracts and uplifts others and creates a safe haven for revealing deepmost feelings, hopes and hurts. Understanding is the golden fruit of wisdom – the wisdom that is produced in your heart from the grafting together of love, knowledge and experience. Understanding is wisdom-in-action, the love-and-life-giving nutrient that is an antidote to the thorny realities of physical life and emotional disappointments. Through understanding, you see others beyond your expectations of them and the roles they play in your life. Through understanding, you realize that your parents were once children, and that they suffered and braved the passages and travails of life in their own ways, just as you have. Understanding gives your romantic partner time, space and self-sovereignty for his or her own individuation. Understanding is an act of kindness that allows others to be who they are in your presence, even if you don't relate to or agree with them or their preferences or behaviors. Understanding extends respect and 'leeway' to loved ones, friends, peers and yourself in circumstances that you actually don't yet, and may never, understand. Ultimately, the willingness to understand paves the way for old harbored 'truths' of resentment and woundedness to emerge and evolve into new lighter and more loving truths, through forgiveness and releasing of the past into brave new present and future dawns.

The willingness to understand is extended to another through receptivity, listening and non-reactionary response. This can be especially difficult when people speak in ways to each other that 'push buttons' and trigger long-standing points of contention and self-esteem issues, especially involving the need for acknowledgment and approval. The key is to listen with heart-awareness to the other person's feelings – even if they seem irrational or accusatory. Listening and even inquiring further of the their feelings, without getting defensive yourself, will allow the tangled and knotted threads of old emotions to unravel. Ultimately, understanding will show both of you that the original causal pain of each lies in your own hearts, and that the other is a mirror to show where healing is needed.

Thus dear one, allow my LELAHEL light of understanding to be magnified within your heart, for your heart's capacity to understand even what cannot be understood is eternally greater than the mind. Through the understanding that is born of your heart's wisdom, you are able to make quantum leaps into whole new horizons of possibility in not only your mutual relatings, but in mutual liberation, lightening and enlightening of each and all. Amen...

3/27 * 6/9 * 8/24 * **11/5** * 1/15

7 ACHAIAH

(a-KA-hee-YAH)
Patience (G)
'One who brings the stillness'
Archangel ~ METATRON
Taurus / Mercury (4/21-25)

I AM THAT WHICH...

helps to cultivate patience and listening in interpersonal dynamics so that learning, compassion and the light of understanding may flourish. Patience is not a discipline of the mind, but a kindness of heart. For it is the heart that is willing to be present to wondering and learning, or to be an ear or a shoulder when someone needs to be heard or felt. It is the heart that helps to coax the depths of another and invite something new that's trying to come forth. The patience of heart understands that all things and beings have their individual attributes and their seasons of becoming more of who they are, each in their own time and way. And it this wise and compassionate patience that is willing to be still and witness the Divine in the self and the other, and share the mutual isness of that profound truth.

Impatience is often an underminer in your relatings with each other. Whether in relatings with loved ones, friends or colleagues, impatience sends an underlying message that the interests or concerns of one are more important than another's, and it shows a lack of willingness to accommodate the other's processes. When parents, teachers and older siblings are chronically impatient with children, the development of their entire beingness can be compromised. For while a child may react angrily, the message imprinted within the child over time is that he or she is not important or worthy of attention. When older children become impatient with elder parents, the same message is sent. The parent begins to feel inconsequential and not needed or respected. When an employer is impatient with an employee, a sense of shame and inadequacy can develop which undermines performance and continues to elicit more impatience. This happens also with 'strangers' – when the young, the old, the infirm, or simply someone having a difficult day, is rushed along or rudely treated. Remember these things when the vehicle in front of you drives slower than the speed limit, or the person in the crosswalk is taking a long time to cross, or someone doesn't understand you at first. You have the power in that moment to grant them dignity by how your energy holds space for the uniqueness of their being and the differences between your individualities.

So please do draw upon my ACHAIAH light within you to amplify your willingness and ability to be patient. For patience is the great respecter of the humanity within each and all. And whenever you do feel impatient, do not let self-judgment distract you from simply entering into your heart, which has all the patience in this and other worlds for your instant appropriation – as many times a day as needed! For the gift of patience among you is to come into the stillness together to know that I Am the Divine within you each and all that patiently awaits you, always, in all ways. Amen...

3/28 * 6/10 * 8/25 * **11/6** * 1/16

8 CAHETEL

(KA-heh-TEL)
Divine Blessings (G)
'One who conducts the flow of plenty'
Archangel ~ METATRON
Taurus / Moon (4/26-30)

I AM THAT WHICH...

helps you to embrace the blessings of family, friendship and community so that the abundant and diverse nature of the Divine within the human might be multiplied and celebrated. The very foundation of life is based on relationship and what can be created and multiplied when two or more are gathered in the growing and sharing of love and beingness. All interpersonal dynamics, including those which are difficult, hold the potential blessings of freedom and expansion for each individual, as well as the whole. The nature of the universe is such that there is truly 'enough to go around.' It is when one takes at the expense of others that the 'distribution' is disturbed. When you individually and collectively think of your relatings together in terms of multiplying abundance rather than dividing, guarding or even hoarding it, then you will see opportunities and fruition flourishing all around you and others. And we do not speak of material blessings only, or even primarily, for this is only a particular fruit of abundance and does not of itself seed the self-replenishing treasures of love, joy and peace that are the source of abundance.

The richer blessings in your relatings with others are those intangibles that cannot be measured, but which make a tangible difference in your well-being and ability to draw abundance in all its forms. These are the shared kindnesses of word and deed, generosity of spirit, co-creative conversation and collaboration, and especially mutual support and encouragement. A word or gesture of support at just the right time – at any age or circumstance – can make all the difference between despair or hope, a dream dared or abandoned, the heart to do and be or not.

Dear blessed one, partake of my light as CAHETEL to see that the blessings of life are constant, and that experiencing them is about entering the flow. You must be immersed in the river of life, not trawling about in the backwaters of fear, doubt, shame, guilt, disappointment, worry or self-judgment, or waylaid on the banks of apathy or lethargy, letting the vibrancy of life pass you by. Immerse, give yourself to life, and open your heart to receive. Allow both ebb and flow to move through you to continually empty out what was in order to fill up again with the new. And if you do become despairing or disheartened for what you seem not to have, may you come gratefully into your heart and work creatively with what you do have and who you are in the goodness and trueness of your deepmost being. See and feel the blessing of life itself, and give thanks that life gives you a new start every day. Be well on the inside, for all things on the outside will pass in order to bring you new gifts. And know this: every time an external resource is depleted, your internal resources can activate the flow again. Draw from my CAHETEL light, for I am the blessings-flow of the Divine streaming through you always, in all ways. Amen...

November 7 – 14

Angels 9 – 16

Sephira 2

CHOKMAH ~ Wisdom

Overlighting Archangel

RAZIEL ~ 'Secrets of God'
Spiritual guidance, keeper of wisdom
and revealer of the mysteries

9 HAZIEL

10 ALADIAH

11 LAUVIAH

12 HAHAIAH

13 YEZALEL

14 MEBAHEL

15 HARIEL

16 HAKAMIAH

9 HAZIEL

(HA-zee-EL)
Divine Mercy and Forgiveness (S)
'One who sees with the light of love'
Archangel ~ RAZIEL
Taurus / Uranus (5/1-5)

I AM THAT WHICH...

helps to facilitate forgiveness and reconciliation in order to free your love to create new life and new ways of relating. Mercy is the compassion of second chances, and forgiveness of self and others is for giving life back to yourself. Only then may there be an opportunity to set things right. Unforgiveness in human life is a complex agreement between harbored pain and the need to punish and remain connected to the offender. However, the harm done in an act of wrongdoing is often much less than the harm of carrying around the burden of unforgiveness day after day, year after year. When unforgiveness is used to stay connected to someone or something, especially in the case of 'rejection,' you deprive yourself of the 'best revenge,' as you say, which is moving on from the husk of the past to the gift of new life and love that awaits you. Be merciful to yourself and find a point of connection in the present which affirms rather than denies the life and beauty within you.

In your relationship with the Divine, there is no need for forgiveness in the human sense because Divine Love cannot be offended and does not regard Its creations as bad or good, wrong or right. These exist as qualifiers only in the realm of duality in which the spiritual and the physical co-exist. We see all your 'wayward' behaviors as the antics of angels with folded wings! And more deeply than that, we see all you do as the striving of your soul to become conscious and expressive in your physicality so that you might ennoble your humanity and do what you are here to do. Every grudge you hold holds you back and weighs you down. If you would see yourselves and each other as we see you, then would you take each other's 'offenses' less personally, then would you more easily see your hurtful behaviors as the acting out of hurting hearts. Then would you more easily feel compassion and mercy and be free to love and be loved.

Thus dear one, call on my HAZIEL light to see yourself and others in the greater light of the soul's longing to be fully alive and fully conscious in physicality. See with the eyes of your heart the greater truth of who you are, and be kind and merciful to yourselves and each other. Feel our love and gratitude within you for so doing, and see our light commingling with yours to compound and help you expand every life-affirming act and moment of grace between and among you. Amen...

3/30 * 6/12 + 13am * 8/27 * **11/8** * 1/18

10 ALADIAH

(a-LA-dee-YAH)
Divine Grace (G)
'One who endows you with the yes of life'
Archangel ~ RAZIEL
Taurus / Saturn (5/6-10)

I AM THAT WHICH...

helps you to bestow grace upon others by seeing the light of love and truth within them and lovingly allowing them to be who they are in your presence without criticism or judgment. This is perhaps the greatest grace you can give to each other – to see each other's light of pure isness and to allow for 'more to the story than meets the eye,' and time and space for it to be revealed. It is a paradox of relationship that the ones you love most are often the most difficult to be unconditionally loving with. This is often because, especially with family, partners and close friends, there are wishes and desires, expectations and sometimes even demands and personal investments in their optimum success and well-being. It is natural and loving to want the ones you love to do and be well. However, when conflict occurs around this, you must ask yourself, do you want for them what they truly want for themselves, or what you think they should want and have – or what you secretly once wanted for yourself, but were not able to achieve or chose differently? No one can live well around those who are always waiting for them to be something more or someone else.

The concept of 'should,' as in what you or someone else should be or do, is a yoke that hangs over your humanity as a by-product of the notion of 'original sin,' and it can seep insidiously into all your attitudes and relatings with yourselves and each other. But it is impossible to live happily 'in the land of should' – whether the 'shoulds' are directed to yourself or to others. You and every being needs some grace-space around you to explore and pursue who you truly are – even when that means journeying down some bumpy and winding roads. Rarely does life go 'as the crow flies' – and indeed, life's most interesting opportunities and 'destiny-events' often happen during detours, delays and unplanned encounters and happenings. For from these come the grace-gifts of coincidence, serendipity and all things magical which give you a sense of knowing and being known by each other, and life itself, in a deeper and larger way.

And so I offer you my ALADIAH light as Divine Grace within you to share with those around you. Be at peace with your own being so that you may be the one others can be themselves with. Be the one they can bring their explorations and 'transgressions' to in order to examine and learn without shame or guilt. Every being needs someone who will give that grace of allowance to their beingness. Who does that for you in your world? Who do you offer that grace to? (Besides your dear four-legged loved ones who are your unconditional loving examples!!) We who are the many-hued Angelic expressions of Divine Light, Love and Truth within you offer you this grace always and forever. May you receive it from us that you may give it to each other freely and nobly. Amen...

3/31 * 6/13pm + 14 * 8/28 * **11/9** * 1/19

11 LAUVIAH

(LO-vee-YAH)
Victory (G)
'One who turns every moment into a win'
Archangel ~ RAZIEL
Taurus / Jupiter (5/11-15)

I AM THAT WHICH...

illuminates oppositional dynamics in relationships as mirrors of your own inner conflict, and helps you to focus on what needs healing within yourself rather than what needs fixing in someone else. In almost all cases, dissension, arguments, resentments – any oppositional relatings with others – are illuminations of your own inner dissent and conflict. You can only 'push each other's buttons' if the buttons are there to push! This is the 'gift' of relational conflict – it is easier to see and work on inner issues when there is an external other to call them out. The opportunity for discovering the cause of and ultimately healing outer dissension is if at least one of you stops reacting and starts asking questions and listening to the answers. Deep down each wants to be heard because you are each needing to hear yourself, which is easier when someone else is listening. However, to persist in arguing and accusing with the goal of being the one who is right, or wronged by the other, may win you the battle – but that win may lose you the war. Meaning that the relationship will become strained and distant. Wherever there is a winner and a loser in an inner or outer battle, a divide persists. Thus, true victory is not possible unless everyone wins. This is just as true in interpersonal dynamics as in business negotiations. If you cut your opponent down in battle, they are not going to enjoy 'getting into bed with you' afterwards!

The same is true for the quality of relatings among all your own inner and outer parts. You must consider what the whole of you needs and wants by listening to each part of yourself. Otherwise, your parts will remain fragmented and alienated from each other as they continue to struggle for dominance – even as your self-conflict continues to be played out externally. For example, an ongoing situation with a family member who always seems to belittle you is perpetuated by a hotspot in each of you. Those who need to belittle others do so because they feel little and need to make others feel small in the hope that they will feel bigger, or at least not smaller. Those who react to being belittled do so because they already feel small inside, and thus it's like 'pouring salt on a wound' or' grease in a hot frying pan.' The only possibility for a win here is for someone to stop accusing, defending or retaliating and drop into the heart to see something good about the other and express it. It's a simple thing really, and such a short distance from one heart to another – but when harbored hurt, pride and anger rule, it can be as the distance to the moon and back.

Thus, I offer you ever so gently the suggestion that when you have difficulty having compassion for yourself, let your compassion for another show you how it's done. And may my LAUVIAH light illuminate this – if you truly want to be a winner, let the other be one too. For in the allness of love and truth, there are no losers in the universe! Amen...

4/1 * 6/15 * 8/29 * **11/10** * 1/20

12 HAHAIAH

(ha-HA-ee-YAH)
Refuge, Shelter (G)
'One who is a beacon of shelter within'
Archangel ~ RAZIEL
Taurus / Mars (5/16-20)

I AM THAT WHICH...

keeps an eternal flame of love and comfort lit in your heart, that you may always find Divine shelter within yourself and offer your heart-shelter to others when a moment of refuge is needed in their lives. In your busy world of demands, responsibilities and daily to-do lists, it can seem challenging to have the time for others on below-surface levels. But one moment of presence with someone in need of attention – by listening, helping, hugging, playing, advising, laughing or crying together – can transcend time. In being present with the other, which also gives you a chance to be present with yourself, you suddenly remember what's important and why it even matters that you do what you do in your life and work. In a moment of heart-opening with your friend, loved one or even a stranger, you re-enact the Divine Love for you and all beings, which has all the time in the world and beyond for receiving you. And in that moment of transcendent time which the present is a gateway to, you are made privy to not only that greater love held within your own inner divinity, but also the boundless resources of the eternal.

In the mysteries of 'where two or more are gathered,' there is always a third invisible presence – a creation energy that is attentive and responsive to need, desire and possibility. When you partake of this presence, there is an enhanced seeing, knowing and feeling available to you. You somehow know just the right thing to say or do for the other. You see what is hidden and hear what has gone unspoken. And you are able to create a momentary 'safe haven' for the baring of heart, mind and soul. And with this, you give the other seeds of love, courage and strength to go back into the details of their lives and do what must be done according to a deeper, newly-revealed truth, in their own time and way.

If you are a 'helper type,' you may need to be especially attentive to your own moments of need. You don't always have to be the strong one – even if it's your gift, purpose or professional work to be a 'go-to' for others. If that's the case, then seek out certain friendships and loved ones with whom you can have mutual listening and exchange, shoulders for leaning, comforting hugs and even some pampering. Commune with colleagues in your work life whose discernment you trust when you have questions and concerns about your life's direction. Be open to the ministering of a stranger who somehow says exactly what you need to hear at just the right moment. Know that each time you ask someone for help, you give them a chance to be of help and to experience a sense of worthwhileness in being valued for their offerings.

And in all these relatings dear one, know that I, HAHAIAH, and all that is Divine, are ministering to you through each other. There is not one moment on your Earth when you are alone and bereft, no matter what the seeming, for you are always being watched over from within and all around you. Just as we dwell within you as your lifelong inner companions, often we help to orchestrate the crossing of paths with those in your world to exchange the light of a smile, a word, a kindness, a comfort, a friendship at just the right moment for either or both of you. And even though some of your relatings may be 'rubbing you the wrong way" – like grains of sand in the oyster, you are helping to turn each other into shining pearls. And it is the grace among you that you may also be each other's refuge just by opening your hearts to what is possible when you are gathered in the willingness of love. For wherever and however you go forth, it is the love and light within you, and that which is shared between and among you, that is your greatest refuge and eternal source of renewal. Amen...

4/2 * 6/16 * 8/30 * **11/11** * 1/21

13 YEZALEL

(YAY-za-LEL)
Fidelity, Loyalty and Allegiance (G)
'One who keeps faith with the inner Divine'
Archangel ~ RAZIEL
Gemini / Sun (5/21-25)

I AM THAT WHICH...

encourages loyalty and sanctity of relationships through familial allegiances, conjugal fidelity, reconciliation and unity, or transcending these when necessary in order to obey a higher order. Family and 'inner circle' friendships compose the foundation and formation of your emotional life. Everything of personal importance you come to do in this life most intimately happens here, in relationship with loved ones and intimates, 'for better or worse.' Thus, whether your relatings are difficult, inhibiting, even potentially harmful – or loving, supportive and encouraging – you 'owe' the formation of your character at least in part to these close personal dynamics. Positive people and relatings become positive examples and role models for the development of character and the cultivation of your individuality. 'Negative' situations and people may serve as examples of who you do not want to be, which can give you additional fervor to become something 'better' or 'more.' Those who use difficult life scenarios to develop strength of character and accomplishment often have an accelerated evolutionary advantage over those who have had an 'easier' time.

All your relationships and interpersonal circumstances are the 'playing fields' for your pre-chosen soul-lessons and purposes. Thus, whatever the quality of your influences, they are soul-gifts of opportunity, and are to be honored as such. What you make of them is your choice. To 'honor thy father and mother' who have been poor exemplars of these is not to condone their behaviors, but to acknowledge the choices of each soul that brought you together into that life situation in order to learn, grow and become true and strong. What you are ultimately honoring and practicing fidelity and allegiance to is who you have become, aided by all the influences that impacted you. In the case of a family situation that has been nurturing and loving, the challenges to your individuation are different. You may feel the weight of expectation and not want to disappoint. You may feel that you need to be like your parents and loved ones in some way, and even compare yourself unfavorably to them. In either case, whether you are from a supportive or challenging foundational family, there will come a time when you need to reject at least some of what you were born to so that you can become your own person. In honoring the exploration and unfolding truths of your own individuation, you will be better able to honor your seminal influences and magnify those that remain relevant and important to you.

Thus, I offer you my unwavering YEZALEL light that you may use all influences in your life to seek and illuminate the truth of yourself and your own becoming – even if loyalty to yourself and your inner Divine calls you to recede from certain familial and earthly loyalties. Yet be grateful for all that ever was, so that your ongoing isness may be expanded and enriched by your own loving and true choices above and beyond. Amen...

4/3 * 6/17 * 8/31 * **11/12** * 1/22

14 MEBAHEL

(MAY-ba-HEL)
Truth, Liberty and Justice (G)
'One who is freed by Truth to set Truth itself free'
Archangel ~ RAZIEL
Gemini / Venus (5/26-31)

I AM THAT WHICH...

helps you to foster truth among interpersonal relatings by allowing the freedom to express feelings, thoughts and preferences, and being willing to encourage each other's unique personalities, gifts and life-paths without harboring hurt, resentment, anger, guilt or shame. One of the truly loving acts that humans can do for each other is to protect and respect the individuation of each, for your greatest life calling is to express the love and truth of who you are. In an atmosphere of love, truth begets truth and more love. Each time one steps out in truth, those near and far are also seeded with truth, and even inspired to let their own truths emerge, in their own way and time. This is why 'group agreements' must be re-examined from time to time, lest they stifle or even imprison the true becoming of individuals. This is important because the true power of a group is in multiplying and magnifying individual power and purpose, not in maintaining the comfort of conformity.

Only in truth can each and all be free. Only in truth can freedom itself evolve to accommodate newly-emerging truths and beingness that enhance the whole. As truth sets you free, truth itself is set free to evolve into new and even 'truer truths.' And this of course is what some groups fear, because the group wants to protect the status quo and its reason for being. The key is for the group to realize that it too must grow so that it does not become a tyranny to its members and ultimately ineffective in its purposes.

The most important thing to understand about truth is that it cannot be a whole truth without love. For truth may reveal the fact of someone's actions, but love tells the whole story of their intent and motivation, the purpose or pain that drives them. Think of this the next time you judge someone – or yourself – based on actions alone. As the fluidity of love tempers truth with mercy, compassion and understanding, what results is a healing justice of truth that no tradition or penal system can serve up.

Thus, dear one, my light as MEBAHEL is given that you might come to know the greater truths of each other which only love can see and feel and tell. Know that any truth you think you hold about another that constricts or limits the possibilities of the other in your presence is a not a living truth, but a fixed and dead truth which can quash life potential in both of you. Allow those around you to tell and be their truths. For lonely is the one who cannot reveal truth of self in a circle of friends and loved ones. So we say this: if you are suffering from a truth untold, and you want to bring it to light between yourself and another – bring your heart into the circle of telling, and we will bring the light. Amen...

4/4 * 6/18 * 9/1 * **11/13** * 1/23

15 HARIEL

(HA-ree-EL)
Purification (G)
'One who uses the light to wash clean'
Archangel ~ RAZIEL
Gemini / Mercury (6/1-5)

I AM THAT WHICH...

helps you to draw from the pure energies of Divine Love and Truth held within your heart so that you might honor and ennoble your earthly relationships, and to clear energies between you that may at times become cloudy or static. Purity in relationship is not about perfection, but a continual willingness to aspire to more compassionate and honest motivations and actions. Purity cultivates and seeks kindness, trustworthiness and straightforwardness without hidden agendas. Purity thrives for the sake of itself within you and with a sincere desire for the trueness and well-being of the other. Purity is that part of your heart which survives adulteration and the trials of time, which is why you cherish it in your children. Through them you may re-experience the innocence that your adult world often seems to deprive you of, which you often secretly mourn.

Exercising purity with others is treating them how you would like to be treated – not necessarily how you have been treated – which is more commonly practiced. Every time you treat another with respect or kindness, you heal a moment in which you were disrespected or treated unkindly.

Each time you acknowledge another, you heal a time when you were unacknowledged, criticized or ignored. Allowing another's honesty without taking offense shows respect for the truth of both of you. Presuming another's innocence of intent does not make you naïve or ignorant, but shows the purity of intent in your own heart. In seeking purity in all your relatings, you do not take offense when you are not treated in kind, but rather trust in purity itself to return all things and beings to their natural good in their own true time. Believing in the essential purity of each and all, you allow the unfolding of love and truth to slough off the barnacles of hardened attitudes and reveal the longing for love and the clear light of truth untainted within.

Thus I, HARIEL, shimmer within you to let you know that your purity still lives, protected in your heart of hearts, where we help you to hold it in safekeeping for those moments when you return to what we of the Divine always know – that you are a child of goodness, a child of love and magnificent light. In that context, may you draw upon my purification energies when you become world-weary and the waters of love and truth between you become muddied and cloudy. Bring whatever is disturbed into the presence of your willing hearts, where we await to attend you with our cleansing light, and in togetherness you will feel your way back to each other in healing and harmony. Dear one, your natural state is one of purity, so come within and receive our Angelic grace that returns you to the knowing that nothing you can do will change that truth. Amen...

4/5 * 6/19 * 9/2 * **11/14** * 1/24

16 HAKAMIAH

(ha-KA-mee-YAH)
Loyalty (G)
'One who aligns with the inner Divine'
Archangel ~ RAZIEL
Gemini / Moon (6/6-10)

I AM THAT WHICH...

helps you to discern how to 'juggle' diverse loyalties among family, close intimates, friends and colleagues with loyalty to yourself and your own truths and inner callings. In your world, the dynamics of emotional and mental liaisons and loyalties can represent some of your most complex challenges. Expectations and the potential for disappointment run at full throttle here, especially when the call of loyalty to others opposes loyalty to self. While family loyalty is a loyalty of heart and blood and considered by many to be sacrosanct, to the soul it is not supreme. When you are asked to do something that goes against your own truth, your values and sense of right, your soul will ask you to choose your own higher ground. This does not make you a betrayer, but rather a stand in your family and relationships for what is true and life-affirming, rather than a complicitor in situations that may be undermining and depleting. If doing so causes you to lose the 'love' of your loved ones, then their love wasn't really love, but self-interest. Preservation of loyalty in family and friendships is short-lived if it must be purchased by wrong-doing or self-betrayal.

Two areas in human life that are often prone to disloyalty are romantic and business partnerships. These are vulnerable because partnership of any kind must always consider and be balanced with the aspirations, dreams and and ambitions of personal individuation. Thus, like family, social and professional groups, a partnership's strength is in its fluidity, not fixity. Personal loyalties are often sacrificed to professional ambitions, just as personal partnerships are often sacrificed to temporary appetites and desires. While marriage and business contracts presume the commitment of individuals to a united whole, the well-being of the members must be sustained in order to maintain the whole. What frequently happens over time, however, is that the commitment becomes a 'governor,' even a taskmaster, in which there is less and less room for individual exploration and growth – to the point that the one who strives to do so can be considered 'selfish' and a threat to the whole.

My light as HAKAMIAH desires to illuminate this – the 'betrayal' is never the desire to explore, run ahead or move on from 'the pack' or partnership. The betrayal is in secrecy, lies and any diminishment or harm to others that you may intentionally cause in order to do so. When you make a stand for alignment with what is true and right in your own heart, though you may disappoint others and even seem to make some enemies, you will also be cultivating allies. For most beings want to have the courage to do what is right and live according to their personal truths and values. Each time one does so, seeds of the same are planted within the hearts and minds of others near and far. So dear one, do choose your loyalties based on what you hold dear, with people who support you in that. Amen...

November 15 – 22

Angels 17 – 24

Sephira 3

BINAH ~ Understanding

Overlighting Archangel

TZAPHKIEL ~ 'Beholder of the Divine'

Understanding of self and God, contemplation,
meditation and compassion

17 LAVIAH

18 CALIEL

19 LEUVIAH

20 PAHALIAH

21 NELCHAEL

22 YEIAYEL

23 MELAHEL

24 HAHEUIAH

17 LAVIAH

(LAH-vee-YAH)
Revelation (R)
'One who parts the veil'
Archangel ~ TZAPHKIEL
Gemini / Uranus (6/11-15)

I AM THAT WHICH...

illuminates that nothing is hidden to the heart that wants to see, and that by seeing each other through the eyes of the heart, your relatings will be deepened as you are each revealed for who you truly are and what you truly feel and want. All revelations happen in the present. In being utterly present you are endowed with a sudden 'direct line' to the greater knowing of the eternal, which is why your 'a-ha' moments have so much power. In your willingness to see and hear and feel the other, love and truth rush in and all is revealed – for no one can resist being loved and listened to.

The importance of love and truth in the dynamics of revelation is this: Truth encompasses the fact, the isness of a being, both eternally and in time. Love is the motivating key and the 'prime mover' toward what more one longs to be. Both of these are needed to reveal and understand the whole story of anyone, including yourself. But first, if you would part the veil to the mysteries of each other, then you must each be willing to take off your blinders.

Blinders are not always made of the obvious 'materials.' Often constructed with threads of fear, worry, doubt, past associations, harbored hurts and resentments, self-interest, stubbornness, pride or greed – they may also be made of noble intentions – a sense of responsibility for the other, a desire for the other's well-being, a well-meaning presumption of what the other needs or wants, or should want, often based on your own values and desires. Taking off your blinders means you are willing for the other person to reveal who they are and what they want without being shunned or 'shut down' by who you are and what you want. In other words, you must love them for their sake, not yours. If this is the case, then blinders begone, and the true and whole-seeing of love can begin!

And so, my brave, naked-hearted, blinderless one, in such willing and courageous moments I am right here with and within you, illuminating for you that whatever may be revealed about the other, you are also being revealed in this moment as the truth of yourself. And know that truly, love will never leave you – for love is a great shapeshifter, coming to you always in changing forms. So be not afraid of hearing another's truth, for love is always in attendance with truth, poised to move truth into ever greater and more loving versions of itself for you and each and all. And know always that whatever truth is sought in you or another, it is always through the light of love that it wants to be seen. Amen...

4/7 * 6/21 * 9/4 * **11/16** * 1/25

18 CALIEL

(KA-lee-EL)
Justice (S)
'One who sustains the cosmic laws of love and truth for all'
Archangel ~ TZAPHKIEL
Gemini / Saturn (6/16-21)

_____

I AM THAT WHICH...

helps to cultivate discernment and a natural sense of justice based on wisdom of heart, the seeking of truth and an integrity that weighs all sides with fairness and compassion. The hearts within all beings hold a sense of justice, from the most to the seemingly least innocent among you. Love's justice for truth's sake seeks fairness, whereas the justice of pride or anger seeks only revenge and punishment for a slight or harm suffered. With love's justice you treat others as you would like to be treated – which may not be how you have been treated. However, you can change the impact and atmosphere of unjust treatment upon you, and be healed of it, by treating others more kindly – even those who have been unjust against you.

Injustice is visited upon most people at one time or another, in small or great ways. It is usually painful, and often causes reactions of anger, resentment and feelings of betrayal or unworthiness – especially in families. However, with love and compassion for self and others, you are able to understand that those who commit injustice are often acting from unresolved hurts and injustice harbored within

95

themselves. As your world's greatest exemplars of love have shown, 'turning the other cheek is a way of meeting injustice with heart. By virtue of your inner divinity you have the intuitive power within your heart to see into the heart of anyone who treats you unfairly and know their hurt.

If you are the transgressor, you will likely feel some degree of shame, self-judgment or guilt. But judging and punishing yourself distracts you from setting things right. True justice is accomplished by using feelings of shame and guilt as an alert to begin corrective action. Transgressions against another occur when you are separated from the love and truth of yourself and the Divine that inhabits your heart and soul. Thus, may the Divine light within your heart help to illuminate the self-transgression that caused your hurt against another, and the path of 'at-onement' that can restore you to integrity and wholeness with yourself and the person you acted against. In the pursuit of justice, love means being willing to say you're sorry and to redeem your actions accordingly.

My CALIEL light offers you this further: though you may seek justice from each other for imagined or real offenses, you will receive full justice only from the natural laws of the cosmos which ever seek the restoration of balance. Every act, 'good' or 'bad,' is revisited upon the actor sooner or later and in one way or another – not as a reward or a punishment, but as the energetic nature of life in which like attracts like and each reaps what is sown. In the eternal story of the soul and its desire for experience and growth, transgressions are opportunities to learn and restore equilibrium through love and righteousness. Thus let your justice to self and others be kind and merciful. Amen...

4/8 * 6/22 * 9/5 * **11/17** * 1/26

19 LEUVIAH

(LOO-vee-YAH)
Expansive Intelligence & Fruition (G)
'One who uses heart to quicken soul memory and expand mind'
Archangel ~ TZAPHKIEL
Cancer / Jupiter (6/22-26)

I AM THAT WHICH...

helps to enhance your relatings and collaborations with others by extending the reach and capacities of your mind through tapping the depth of your heart and its vast resources of feeling, insight, intuition and wisdom. An expansive intelligence is one that is able to experience quantum leaps in processing information beyond 'facts and figures' to encompass underlying aspects, patterns of interconnectivity and non-linear knowing from the eternal realms. This is the kind of quantum intelligence which happens with visionaries in any field who are able to think outside the usual boxes in which the mind compartmentalizes information. For example, when you are able to comprehend that art, science and spirituality do not refute or conflict – but illuminate, elaborate upon and even 'prove' each other. In the context of relationship, this quantum effect is multiplied when the resources of multiple hearts and minds are working in tandem and begin to cross-pollinate and inspire new discoveries, revelations and co-creations that none could have created on their own.

The use of your soul-memory is key to how much of your heart and mind is available for being present, insightful and co-creative in relationship and collaboration with others. If your 'memory banks' are taken up with past events, disappointments, grievances, harbored hurts, resentments, anger, pride, shame and so on, then the range and use of your intelligence can be compromised. The more emotionally healed you are, the more mental clarity you have because there is less emotional sludge to 'gunk up the works!' Your inner lines of communication will have less static and you will be more able to tune into the time and place where anything you need to know emerges, which of course, is the present –- which then gives you access to the super-reality of the eternal and the ability to draw from universal all-knowing.

Thus my light as LEUVIAH is given to help you expand your intelligence by being fully present in all your relatings so that your mind's memory functions will operate at optimum levels in these ways: to discern and tap into interconnections and patterns of all events from multiple timelines and 'information downloads' that are relevant to present happenings, and to have access to the greater knowing of intuition, wisdom and universal energies that emerge only in moments of full presence, which can amplify 'ancient-future' memory. In these ways, dear expanded one, your heart-powers and mental faculties work together to amplify and increase the quality of all your relatings and co-creations. Thus may you go forth with each other unencumbered, that you are free to make so much more of yourselves in togetherness. Amen...

4/9 * 6/23 * 9/6 * **11/18** * 1/27

20 PAHALIAH

(pa-HA-lee-AH)
Redemption (G)
'One who restores the self'
Archangel ~ TZAPHKIEL
Cancer / Mars (6/27-7/1)

I AM THAT WHICH...

illuminates that your true 'redeemer' is the Spirit of Love that proceeds from the inner divinity of your heart and soul, which helps you to make choices that support the 'redemption' of your own life and those around you – and even the generations before and after you. There exist sayings and stories in your holy books and literatures about how 'the sins of the patriarchs shall be visited upon the children...but the children shall redeem them.' This speaks of three great mysteries about sowing and reaping: First, the cosmic (natural) law of 'like attracts like' causes the reaping in kind of whatever has been sown. Secondly, however, by virtue of your inner divinity you have available to you the grace to bring forth a different fruit than what was sown in you by yourself or others. Thirdly, in doing so you may redeem (as in 'reclaim') yourself from the law of sowing and reaping by the grace to end your suffering and thus no longer pass it on. In being freed from the legacies of harm and hurt, you also to a certain extent redeem those who did the initial doing and those present and future others who, like ripples in a pond, might have still been impacted.

It is the 'savior-self' within you that will 'save' yourself, by allowing the Divine within to heal your offenses and wash you clean of any impulse of unkindness to yourself or others. Thus you will do unto others not what was done to you, but something new and good that comes from your own freed will and reborn heart. Your 'redeemer' is within you – not outside of you, 'above' in the heavens or back in the histories of man. Your inner redeemer is the living presence of Divine Love – by whatever name it was and ever is called – empowering you to become the full Divine-Human being that you truly are. The power of love in form is that it offers you tangible, knowable and visible relating. But while forms in your reality fall and fade away, the Spirit of Love lives on eternally and dwells in every heart, mind, soul, body and being that ever comes to be. The part you play in your own redemption is in awakening to it and welcoming it by offering the softer side of your own will, which is willingness, to the sacred act of receiving.

Thus I, PAHALIAH, am given to you for this – to not be bound by the circumstances you were born into or the pain that was inflicted upon you yesterday or 'seven generations' ago. You can reclaim yourself from the past by receiving the Divine-Human fullness of yourself in the present. Forgive those who came before you, that your forgiveness may give your life back to you and allow only love and truth their rightful sovereignty within you. Endow your new 'second birth' and bearing upon all you love and care for, all your friends and all you meet, so that the light-seeds of their own inner redemptions might be stirred and sprouted. Allow the Spirit of Love to do its work within you, and the whole and greater truth of your beauties will be revealed. Amen...

4/10 * 6/24 * 9/7 * **11/19** * 1/28

21 NELCHAEL

(NEL-ka-EL)
Ardent Desire to Learn (G)
'One who inspires delight in learning'
Archangel ~ TZAPHKIEL
Cancer / Sun (7/2-6)

I AM THAT WHICH...

helps you to open your heart to the realization that the potential of your relationships can be endless when you are continually interested in learning about the other and exploring the wonder of your differences, as well as the sameness of heart beneath them. Relationships of all kinds – especially partnerships, families and friendships – have the most longevity and highest quality of relating when the individuals realize that there is always something new to learn about each other. Often when you have known someone a long time, you may assume you know everything there is to know about them. This is partly a way to create a comfort level in being with each other, but it also shows an unwillingness to 'dive into the depths', and is a shallow presumption upon the other that serves neither of you. If you begin to explore the other's heart, mind and soul, then you realize there is a vastness which you could spend your entire life and beyond exploring. It is staying on the surface in your relatings that eventually bores you and can cause you to continually seek out others. But that is a numbers game – a game of quantity and superficiality – not quality or depth.

In depthful relating, there is no end to not only what you can learn about each other, but what your continued interest can help to catalyze, reveal and inspire in the other. And by individual and mutual discovery of self and other, there is no end to what you can explore and co-create in the world around you. Ask each other questions without assuming you already know the answer – and listen to what emerges. Query and explore expecting to see, hear and find something new, for indeed all beings are always evolving and growing. Anyone who seems not to be is someone who no one is showing sufficient interest in to awaken the richness of who they are.

And so, dear interesting and interested one, take on my NELCHAEL mantle of illuminating light to open your all-seeing heart and learn about the others in your life. Start with the one who is most 'stereotypical' to you, the one you know least about but perhaps presume the most. Do not be put off if their initial answers are shallow or resistant, for perhaps they are not used to being plumbed. If you continue to beam upon them your light of interest, they will begin to call up from within what is interesting about them that they didn't even know themselves. You have the power to do this for each other – to show each other your magnificence, so that you might know and feel the worthiness of your Divine-Human beingness. Thus, awaken each other's hearts, minds and souls and partake of the eternal within you – and thereby lighten your world with your beautiful glows of mutual and self-discovery. We so love this capacity within you that in any moment 'where two or more are gathered' thusly, we are especially quickened to attend and amplify the gathering light! Amen...

4/11 * 6/25 * 9/8 * **11/20** * 1/29

22 YEIAYEL

(YAY-ah-YEL)
Fame, Renown (G)
'One who seeks knowing of self'
Archangel ~ TZAPHKIEL
Cancer / Venus (7/7-11)

I AM THAT WHICH...

helps you to appreciate the uniqueness and talents of others in ways that inspire you to use your own gifts and successes to express and expand your true self and purposes. Each of you is the 'star of your own show' in a reality of your own making. There are many who are 'famous' among you – as actors, artists, scientists, innovators, entertainment personalities, educators, politicians, princes, kings, and ordinary people doing extraordinary things. And they impact your world and your individual psyches in many ways. While those who enjoy renown are often entertaining and inspiring, you must be able to appreciate their uniqueness without appropriating their reality as yours. It may be that when you are striving for your own sense of identity and purpose, or you admire someone else's gift and desire to learn from them, you may emulate and learn from others for a time. Through the ages, your creations have been influenced and inspired by each other in wondrous ways. But ultimately, you are each an original. You cannot successfully be anyone else, so why not be the one no one else can be! For you are not fully alive if you live vicariously through the fame and success of others. Rather, let the 'stars' among you – who are shining with their own unique dreams, talents and purposes – inspire you to pursue the gifts, dreams and desires of your own heart. And then your likeness to them will be that you too are unique and wondrous in the powers of your making and becoming!

Let my light as YEIAYEL remind you of this whenever you have even a splinter of thought that someone else's life is more valuable than yours: Admire each other without pedestals and idolizing. Learn from each other, inspire each other, help each other and be glad for each other's successes for their own sake, knowing at the same time that nothing truly succeeds that 'copies' or depends upon the success or failure of others. Rather let the success of each add to and inspire the fullness of the whole. The most important message that any person with a podium of fame, prestige or accomplishment can impart to the world is to be the best of your own true and unparalleled self. Realize that each of you expresses a unique aspect of the Divine Being and Nature – a particular puzzle piece of Creation needed to fill out that magnificent 'bigger picture' of All That Is. Thus, no one is inconsequential. The physical life of your soul is an opportunity to grow the seeds of potential for your own greater expression, as well as to root and diversify the Divine on Earth through your unique growth and creations. The key to this, dear beloved, is that you must live your own life, your own dreams and passions – follow the star in the sky of your own heart, not someone else's. Amen...

4/12 * 6/26 * 9/9 * **11/21** * 1/30

23 MELAHEL

(MAY-la-HEL)
Healing Capacity (G)
'One who shows where healing is possible'
Archangel ~ TZAPHKIEL
Cancer / Mercury (7/12-16)

I AM THAT WHICH...

helps to amplify your capacity to support healing in your relationships by the willingness to approach with heart – without conditions, demands, hopes or expectations. Every hurting place in a relationship is ultimately not meant to bring pain, but to show where healing is needed in each of you and between you. Drawing on the resources of your heart – love, insight, compassion, forgiveness and wisdom – you are better able to accept who the other is now, even while they are striving to become 'more.' You will sense whether a comforting shoulder, or time and space, is needed for their own self-exploration. You will be able to listen in a way that enables you to hear not only what is said, but what longs to be – and provide a 'safe' atmosphere in which confidences and revelations may come forth without needing to compare their feelings or choices to yours. If the relationship between you needs healing, you will be able to acknowledge and allow their feelings even if your own feel endangered. For with love, a healing truth will emerge, and even have the life-affirming potential to change into a new truth.

Sometimes healing can be done together, and sometimes the healing, or some of it, must be done separately. In that case, love for the truth of oneself and the other must be greater than the fear of loss, for only with unconditional love is healing possible. If you let someone go in love and peace, it gives them room to make the return journey in their own true time. And if there is a final parting of ways, then the love that was will still remain to take new forms, in the right and true time.

And so dear one, let your heart be filled with my MELAHEL light so that healing in the right and true way for each other shall be forthcoming for the highest good. Dare to love, and the truth of each of you will emerge in a way that is most loving. Love, and love will carry you through loss, change and every new horizon that awaits you. Love, no matter what, even as the Divine loves you, always and forever, with no conditions, no demands, no exceptions – and healing will come, with greater understanding and a path forward that increases the life of each who walk it, individually and together. Amen...

4/13 * 6/27 * 9/10 * **11/22** * 1/31

24 HAHEUIAH

(ha-HOO-ee-YAH)
Protection (G)
'One who is the keeper of true-selfness'
Archangel ~ TZAPHKIEL
Cancer / Moon (7/17-22)

I AM THAT WHICH...

helps you to protect resiliency in your relationships by cultivating an atmosphere of kindness and respect, so that when misunderstandings or offenses arise there is a possibility for hearts to meet and healing to occur. Your most potent protections against hurt and disappointment in your relatings are the life-affirming energies of love and truth carried in your heart, and to trust that all things happen for the ultimate good and growth of all involved. When you act against each other in some way you are usually aware of it and experience a sense of guilt, shame or discomfort quickly after the offense. This is a natural and protective trigger of conscience to address the offense before it begins to fester. Sometimes, however, an offense occurs that is not intended or realized by the offender. And perhaps the one offended says nothing, but harbors a sense of hurt or anger. If the hurt stays hidden, so does all possibility of healing. So your protection is not to close off, but to open to each other. Things erupt on the surface because they want to be healed, and it is your willingness to do so which protects you and your relationships from ongoing harm.

In another light, protectiveness is something you naturally feel for loved ones. The barometer for when responsibility crosses over into over-protectiveness is when the other starts to become afraid because of your fear. While a certain amount of caution is prudent in your world, nothing can hold a candle to the inner-light fortifications of the heart. Over-protective attitudes, talismans, icons and other 'accessories' can accumulate the vibrations of fear and attract that which you are trying to ward off. Better to expand the light than to protect against the 'dark.'

My protective light as HAHEUIAH is not to keep hurtful things from happening to you that are part of your soul purposes, but to help you use anything hurtful to learn and create life-affirming outcomes. Thus, I invite you to draw upon my light to meet your challenges in an atmosphere of compassion, honesty, humility and the willingness to allow a reconciling light to illuminate the sameness that lives within your hearts. This inner sameness – the desire to love and be loved and to have meaning and worthwhileness in your relatings – is ultimately what protects you from alienation and isolation. By allowing the light of the Divine to amplify your own heart-light, you will not harbor the resentment or unforgiveness which can contaminate your whole being and the relationship. If you bring our commingled light unto the other, healing will quicken. Even if the other person is not able to meet you at that moment, your own willingness has planted a light seed in the other's heart that will sprout when his or her own inner conditions are optimum. So go forth dear one, and be not afraid, for we are always here watching over you from within. Amen...

November 23 – 30

Angels 25 – 32

Sephira 4

CHESED ~ Love/Mercy

Overlighting Archangel

TZADKIEL ~ 'Justice of God'
Mercy and kindness, beneficence,
grace, transmutation

25 NITH-HAIAH

26 HAAIAH

27 YERATEL

28 SEHEIAH

29 REIYEL

30 OMAEL

31 LECABEL

32 VASARIAH

25 NITHAIAH

(NIT-ha-YAH)
Spiritual Wisdom and Magic (R)
'One who quickens the abracadabra of life'
Archangel ~ TZADKIEL
Leo / Uranus (7/23-27)

I AM THAT WHICH...

stirs up the sparkling energies of uncanny coincidence, magical connections and soul-orchestrated encounters between and among you. There are so many ways in which beings relate to each other, and you are likely very aware in your own life which relatings and relationships energize you and which don't. Many interpersonal dynamics stay on the surface to report facts, news, the latest gossip, off-the-cuff opinions and advice, instructions, schedules, to-do lists and so on. Some of these are functional and necessary to daily life, and some are just ways to fill time or silence without getting too involved. However, any magic in your relatings with others involves being fully present with heart and mind, asking real questions and listening for real answers, and welcoming mutual discovery and wonder of feelings, intuitions and new ideas.

With this potency of presence, no one 'disappears' – indeed, as each person is more fully seen by the other, the truths, passions and potentials of each more and more appear. In this heightened vibrancy of co-creative relating, wisdoms and quantum knowing can emerge in the magical way they do 'where two or more are gathered' in inquisitive awareness and mutual recognition. Here and now, in this kind of heart-quickening atmosphere, you have the power to conjure eternity within time and the crackling presence of infinite possibility!

Simply put, here is where inspiration rushes in and everyone involved gets to feel the magnificent 'what a rush!' of creation energy coursing through you. This is the light, the glow, the high of the Divine being fully alive in the Human and of life being fully lived. This is the spiritual magic of being created anew within yourself and with each other by that same creation energy from which all your creations and co-creations are born. These are the moments when you can actually feel the heavens on Earth and their points and patterns of interconnection!

But as you often wonder, how do you hold on to these moments, to the magic?

My light-magic as NITHAIAH tells you this. Moments are made to change, and sustaining this magical quality of life is not about holding on to it or keeping it at the same pitch, but continually renewing it. And to do that, you must again and again return your beingness to the moment, to become heartfully present with yourself and with the other. For it is here in your eternal heart and soul where you will always find us – working 'the stagecraft behind the scenes.' As soon as you show up with your heartful enthusiasm, we are all aflurry and aflutter and ta-daaa! So dear wonder-hearted one – again and again, with every new day and from one moment to the next, let the magic begin! Amen...

4/15 * 6/29 * 9/12 * **11/24** * 2/2

26 HAAIAH

(HA-ee-YAH)
Political Science and Ambition (R)
'One who encourages cooperative expression'
Archangel ~ TZADKIEL
Leo / Saturn (7/28-8/1)

I AM THAT WHICH...

helps you to know who you value in your life, and how to honor and respect those important relationships while pursuing your aspirations and ambitions. You likely have several inner and outer circles of loved ones, friends and colleagues who each play a particular role in your personal, community and work life. Your collective relationships form a kind of 'polis,' a social group organized around what matters to you, who you were born to and who you have chosen to experience different aspects of your life with. Some compose the core and constant in your personal world, and others come and go and play strategic central and peripheral roles in different realms of your interests, aspirations and work. The paradox is that the people in your innermost circle – those who mean the most to you – are often the ones you spend the least amount of time with! And you may justify this with a belief that your ambitions and strategic relationships are for their benefit according to what you feel or assume is best for them. If you were to directly ask them, however, they might have different ideas about that.

A disconnect between who and what you value and how your actions and interactions support those values is very common in your world. This is understandable because you are always juggling all the aspects of your life at the same time – your spiritual, emotional, mental and physical beingness and circumstances, and all the people and purposes that relate with these different parts of you. And you're often pulled by the loudest and most urgent demands. But just like any 'city', populous or social group, there must be a hierarchy of leadership, an inner governor that brings you back to what and who are truly important – and how and when you need to meet the moment with any of them.

My light as HAAIAH is given to help you reorient your attention, actions and ambitions with your truest self according to the loves and truths in all aspects of your life and relatings. Again and again, start with your heart and let it be your governor so that your feeling, intuition and wisdom therein can help you to align all the rest. Start with your heart, and you will access your inner Divine co-creators and the greater knowing that we help to illuminate. Start with your heart, and wherever else you wind up or however you may at times feel lost in the cacophonies and confusions of demands and responsibilities, your heart will find you and bring you back to the why of everything you do and aspire to. Start with your heart, dear one, more and more – until it becomes the alpha and omega of your own beingness. Amen...

4/16 + 17am * 6/30 * 9/13 * **11/25** * 2/3

27 YERATEL

(YEH-ra-TEL)
Propagation of the Light (S)
'One who grows the light with love'
Archangel ~ TZADKIEL
Leo / Jupiter (8/2-6)

I AM THAT WHICH...

expands the light within you to shine through you and upon others the warmth of welcoming, appreciation, kindness and heightened consciousness. You experience light in different ways all day long, because light expresses itself differently according to its 'medium.' Perhaps most obviously, the sun on your side of the world gives you warmth, nurturing and light of day, and in its brief absence the radiance of the moon and stars. In addition to these, of course, your world is a proliferation of light conduction from electrical and mechanical sources. But most importantly, you and every being are light-sources and conductors for yourselves and each other. While the light of joy may be expressed universally as smiles, laughter, enthusiasm, encouraging words, lively physical movements, a sparkle in your eyes, and even tears – each being's expression of light will be unique. Which is why you remember a person's particular smile or words or way. The light of welcoming has an immediate and powerful effect to make you feel not only the warmth of kindness and belonging, but that you are valued, respected and cared about.

Light also expresses between and among you as qualities of consciousness which are conveyed through color, vibratory presence and enlightened expressions of soul, heart, mind and body. Light is the pervasive, ever-evolving shimmer of the Universe and is infinitely revealing, expansive, spreadable, inspiring and life-giving. But just as in the case of undifferentiated white light, none of these 'hues,' or qualities, of light, would be visible without the prism of 'hue-manity!' Light needs all of you in order to reveal and expand the full spectrum of consciousness and the differentiated qualities of Divine Love and Truth which have rendered each of you in a particular 'image and likeness' of the Divine. Through your diversified individuations of 'hue-man' beingness and purpose, and also the ways in which your hearts come together in love, awareness and unity, you continually increase the radiance of light as life unto the world and even the cosmos.

And so, dear light-wand that you are in your unique isness and potentialities, my YERATEL light is grounded within you that you may ever draw from my endless fountain to increase and convey light unto others. On your darkest day of forgetting your light nature, receive another's smile and return your own. Then you may be re-ignited into remembering the light-being that you are and your intrinsic power to light the world and be lit wherever you are and in whatever circumstances. For you hold the light-seeds in your heart that your soul endowed you with when you were born. And as they crack open in every crack of a smile and sparkle in your eyes, let your own Divine-Hueman beingness declare to the cosmos, 'indeed, let there be light!' Amen...

4/17pm + 18 * 7/1 * 9/14 * **11/26** * 2/4

28 SEHEIAH

(say-HAY-ee-YAH)
Longevity (G)
'One who extends life with creation energy'
Archangel ~ TZADKIEL
Leo / Mars (8/7-12)

I AM THAT WHICH...

helps you to come together in love and forgiveness to generate life-affirming energies that can dissolve the stress of daily life, pent-up emotions and harbored hurts. There is nothing that positively impacts your health more than the healing of emotions. During the times when families and friends gather to celebrate holidays and special occasions, it is natural that unresolved issues are stirred up if you hold in your heart a wish or vision of togetherness that your reality contradicts. As painful as this can be, these unrequited desires for more loving interaction can begin to be fulfilled if at least one person goes out on a limb in his or her heart to simply BE more loving. That person could be you. For if not you, then who? If you dare to transform the cycles of reaction into new action, based on what you desire to create **now** *rather than what was uncreated in the past, then the hearts and lives of all involved have an opportunity for healing and rejuvenation.*

There is a mistaken, but commonly held sense, that harboring resentment and anger from old hurts punishes the offender. And although this can perhaps energetically affect

117

the other in negative ways, harbored negative emotions within you will most certainly diminish the light of your own true nature and your interconnections with all others – as well as impede the natural flow of life, love and well-being in everything you aspire to. You may decline into fatigue, lethargy, depression, disease and even a shortened lifespan. That said, both positive and negative emotions are natural to the evolution of your human beingness and the complex dynamics of ebb and flow that advance you through the seasons of life and the cycles of change. The life-affirming key here is to tap the positive potential of negative emotions and interactions by recognizing them as signals, or symptoms, of something that needs to be healed. Love, compassion and forgiveness for self and others, as we say again and again, is for giving you and your life back to yourself. And each time you give life to yourself and yourself to life, you enliven your relationships.

I, SEHEIAH, am here to help you use negative interactions as a gift of illumination. Thus, when you hold any hurt or difficulty up to the all-seeing light in your heart, you will be able to better follow the tangled threads of thoughts and feelings to discern where and what healing is needed and tap our Angelic resources of love and compassion for doing so. And so, dear eternal-souled one, invite 'your others' to meetings of the heart, and wait in your heart for the other's heart to attend. If you bring willingness, we will bring the greater light for both and all to see by – that you may know how to go on and on together! Amen...

4/19 * 7/2 * 9/15 * **11/27** * 2/5

29 REIYEL

(RAY-ee-YEL)
Liberation (G)
'One who liberates the Love and Truth of you'
Archangel ~ TZADKIEL
Leo / Sun (8/13-17)

I AM THAT WHICH...

helps truths to be heartfully revealed so that you may be free to be who you truly are individually and together, and also that old hidden and hurting truths may become free to evolve into new truths and new life energies. It is common to hold back from others your own truths of being, feeling or perception. Sometimes when a personal truth is evolving, you need some private inner space for things to 'process' and for new awarenesses to coalesce. At other times you may hold back or modulate your truth so as not to cause discomfort or hurt to others or disrupt the status quo. Sometimes you may hold back because you are denying it to yourself. And sometimes a harbored hurt will hold truths back as a kind of subconscious 'revenge' or punishment of another. And so dear one, we say to you these things about the power of truth to set you, and even truth itself, free...

No matter what it is, every truth revealed has the power to heal and free the greater potentials of all concerned – even though the revelation may be initially disruptive, difficult or painful. Only lies and unspoken truths which fester and ooze with ongoing woundedness leave scars.

119

'Truth be told,' when you begin to let go of an old truth by expressing it, you are no longer held hostage by it. Instantly you are unbound by the greater truth of a boundless love and its infinite creation energy that always brings more life into the newness of the present and the potency of newly possible truths.

My light as REIYEL lives in your heart to remind you that your heart is your truth-teller. Let the truths that are born inside you, as you, have their light of day, their voice, their reach and 'a leg to stand on.' And may you also allow others the freedom to live their truths in your presence, so thus you may come to know that what is true for another is an opportunity for a deeper truth of your own to make itself known. For in truth, every time your generosities of love, compassion and forgiveness free others to be who they are, you free yourself as well. Thus dear truth-hearted one, be not afraid to feel truth, hear truth, know truth, speak truth and be truth – but always through love, that the whole truth may be forthcoming. Amen...

4/20 * 7/3 * 9/16 * **11/28** * 2/6

30 OMAEL

(O-ma-EL)
Fertility, Multiplicity (G)
'One who loves life into being'
Archangel ~ TZADKIEL
Leo / Venus (8/18-22)

I AM THAT WHICH...

fosters the proliferation of creative energies and enthusiastic interaction among family, friends and peers through the fertile exchange of ideas, thoughts and feelings. It is the inherent urge of your individuality to be creative and expressive in order to bring more of your inner imaginings into outer manifestation. Multiply this times two or more beings, and creative potential is exponentially compounded – especially in collaborations where you 'spark' or 'stoke' each other's ideas and imaginations. Inspire among you 'thinking outside the box,' 'coloring outside the lines,' and generally turning any kind of fodder into a feast of co-creativity. In this vibrant atmosphere where curiosities and explorations abound, there is a shared wonder and magical sense that 'anything is possible.'

This kind of interaction is infinitely more potent than just reporting the facts of your day or your life. It's about plumbing the depths for the riches of meaning and metaphor, signs, synchronicities and new awarenesses. This is how 1 x 1 can = 3 – because any time two come together in openness and co-creativity, a third joins as a co-creative presence that helps to deepen your perceptions and heighten your understandings. This 'presence' is the creation energy of love, which increases and extends your creative powers. It is this same creation energy which attends the physical commingling of two to bring forth a third being from their joining. The key is to keep the aliveness flourishing between and among you.

Often with partners, families and long-time friends there is more emphasis on day-to-day functioning and tasks that must get done. Familiarity and proximity can make you forget that everyone is continually changing and growing inwardly and outwardly. Thinking you know who each other are because you are always there, or here, you can forget to bring your deeper thoughts and curiosities to the other. You may do less seeing, asking and listening. This is often why new friendships become compelling, because you are seen anew – not as who you always were, but who you are now and what more you may even feel inspired to become in their presence and 'new-seeing' of you.

Thus, fertile-one, while treasuring your heart-home of loved ones and the comfort of 'letting your hair down,' use my OMAEL light to see with fresh eyes the ones who have always been there, and dare to look more deeply into their hearts. Be open to new ways of relating, as well as new encounters, that can keep you fresh with yourself and each other. Allow the magic of 'cross-pollination' between the 'old' and the new so that all your relatings may benefit from new life-affirming energies. Share co-creative presence, conversation and adventures! Go forth and multiply each other in the vibrancies of love and truth and full-aliveness! Amen...

4/21 * 7/4 + 5am * 9/17 * **11/29** * 2/7

31 LECABEL

(LAY-ka-BEL)
Intellectual Talent (G)
'One who puts all the pieces together'
Archangel ~ TZADKIEL
Virgo / Mercury (8/23-28)

I AM THAT WHICH...

helps to invigorate interpersonal relatings with co-creative conversation and explorations that stimulate fresh perspectives, innovative ideas and mutual growth. Have you ever noticed that you seem to be 'smarter' and more creative in the company of some people? People with whom you're not just reporting what you know, but where new ideas emerge and flow easily between you, and you create or think of things together that you might not have come up with on your own? And even if your interests and work are very different, you discover areas that are translatable or complementary – adding perspective and versatility to the knowledge and expertise of each of you. And your time together creates a 'glow' and sense of being recharged.

This enthuiastic intellectual sharing may happen more easily with your work colleagues and new friendships, because you generally don't have long-term emotional investments or fixed judgments about each other. However, continually bringing this quality of relating to life partners, family and long-time friendships fosters new levels of

123

communication, growth and enjoyment to each of you as individuals, and to the growth and well-being of the whole.

Sometimes there will be one or more in a family or friendship group who will strike out on their own, go to school far away, move to another town, get a job in the 'big city' or even another country, and then come home for important gatherings and holidays. This can infuse new energy and inspiration, and even vicarious enjoyment of the other's adventures. Sometimes, however, resentment and jealousy may come from those who are unhappy with their own lives. This deprives everyone of the sparkle and inspiration of the new and a free-flow of sharing and mutual learning – but most hurtfully it erodes a sense of belonging. The person who 'colors outside the lines' of the group is potentially the hope of its members. For the light blazing within one is an awakener of the light within each that can 'fire-up' long-held dreams and potentials.

And so, may my LECABEL light be dispersed within and among you that you may each cultivate, appreciate and thereby increase your unique intellects and talents. See and welcome vibrancy from every direction that you may each and all rise up to your greater possibilities and become inspirations to each other. And whatever your talents and proclivities for the new or the familiar, remember that life creates all hues of 'huemankind!' Be glad for those who amplify yours, and also for the rest of the rainbow, who in their unique ways are all important to the sparkle in the tapestry of your life! Amen...

4/22 * 7/5pm + 6 * 9/18 * **11/30** * 2/8

32 VASARIAH

(va-SAH-ree-YAH)
Clemency and Equilibrium (G)
'One who balances judgment with mercy'
Archangel ~ TZADKIEL
Virgo / Moon (8/29-9/2)

I AM THAT WHICH...

helps you to develop a noble heart that sees the positive potential in every thing, circumstance and being and is willing to give wide berth to the seeming transgressions of others so that they may have the time and space to set things right. Whenever you show mercy and compassion to someone who has acted wrongly against you or another, you offer a grace to the other in which something healing and transformative can happen. This 'grace-space' allows the person to realize their transgression and feel genuine remorse, rather than triggering a 'survival instinct' to self-protect against your judgment. You can see this dynamic most simply between partners or parents and children when a transgression is met with silence or stillness rather than instant reaction and recrimination. In that breath of space, the other person can hear his or her own hurtful words. In the lack of accusation, the offender accuses himself. In the absence of punishment, the wrong-doer seeks a way to atone. In the light of compassion and mercy, the person who causes hurt hurts more and feels more readily the need to heal and be healed.

The key to living in a loving and compassionate atmosphere isn't to not hurt each other, but being willing to allow healing to take place – and also to cultivate the personal sovereignty that comes with not taking the actions of others too personally. By not receiving what another does to you, his or her action is 'returned to sender' instantly without compounding it with your reaction. In this way, you do not take on a yoke of ever-accumulating and potentially long-harbored hurts. And in a non-accusative atmosphere, both are better able to communicate without defensiveness toward mutual understanding and healing.

You come here in part to 'rub up against each other' so that you may slough off your rough inner and outer 'edges' and enable your soul-light to shine through your humanity. While harmonious relatings are inspiring and comforting, your difficult encounters are often those which most accelerate and deepen your learnings. And so dear ones, you who bang up against each other's heads and hearts, hurts and hopes, use my VASARIAH mercy-light to be generous in your forgivings. See the more whole truth of yourselves in your sameness of heart beneath your disagreements and differences. Do not let your judgments linger, and let love and heart-wisdom be the pardoner that lightens all transgressions. For in the eyes of the Angels, you are all Divine-Human light-seeds in the fields of time, ever seeking true and loving fruition individually and together. Amen...

December 1 – 8

Angels 33 – 40

Sephira 5

GEBURAH ~ Strength & Judgment

Overlighting Archangel

CHAMAEL ~ 'Severity of God'
(Also CHAMUEL or KAMAEL)
Change, purification and clearing of karma
for stronger loving and nurturing relationships

---

33 YEHUIAH

34 LEHAHIAH

35 CHAVAKIAH

36 MENADEL

37 ANIEL

38 HAAMIAH

39 REHAEL

40 YEIAZEL

33 YEHUIAH

(vay-HOO-ee-YAH)
Subordination to Higher Order (R)
'One who calls you to higher ground'
Archangel ~ CHAMAEL
Virgo / Uranus (9/3-7)

I AM THAT WHICH...

helps you to respect and honor those who came before you for their legacies and contributions to your life, even in striving to surpass them, and to allow dynamics in relationships to shift when love and truth call you down a different path. There are always inner and outer hierarchies of respect and priority in human life, and the 'ruling order' is naturally shifted by new awarenesses, desires, demands and responsibilities at different stages and times. In actuality, you are prioritizing people, demands and desires all day long. Ultimately, the possibility to evolve in a way that is true and healthy for you and those around you is for your 'higher order' to be determined inwardly by what is most consistently true for you and what you most love and value.

As you journey through your life, your truths and priorities will change – for example, when you shift your attention and involvement from your parents and siblings to your own partner and family. However, sometimes this shift must occur much earlier because of the absence of parents or difficult situations in the home that call you to awaken to an inner higher authority so that you might survive your surroundings, and ultimately overcome and surpass them. This is early and brave training for what all must learn eventually, which is to organize your outer hierarchies of importance in alignment with an inner sense of what is most true and purposeful for you.

Following your own 'higher calling' at any age is not easy, because it can mean leaving things and people behind in some way or another. But however difficult, it is less so than living a life of conflict in which you are continually 'serving two masters' when others expect something from you that is different from what you want for yourself. Choosing your own truth does not mean that you do not honor others. In fact, your only hope for healthy relatings with others is born of honoring yourself and your own values first – 'to thine own self be true' so that you may 'do unto others' what is right and true.

Thus, dear brave exploring one, my YEHUIAH light is given unto you so that you might cross the threshold of every higher-order initiation stronger and more full of the love and truth of who you are. In a world that sparkles and glitters with interesting things, people and experiences, as well as demands and responsibilities, it is easy for the seeing of your inner guiding light to be dimmed by so much outward looking. But this light – which is your own soul-light, commingled with the light of all who angelically attend you as your inner Divine Allies – is always with and within you as a beacon and cosmic compass. By our shared light you may locate your personal 'true north' to find your way back to yourself and what matters most to you. Thus you may come to know which way to go and how to be in your world with others in true and right relationship. Amen...

4/24 * 7/8 * 9/20 + 21am * **12/2** * 2/10

34 LEHAHIAH

(lay-HA-hee-YAH)
Obedience (R)
'One who amplifies inner authority'
Archangel ~ CHAMAEL
Virgo / Saturn (9/8-12)

I AM THAT WHICH...

helps you to be obedient to the authorities in your life whose purposes have your best interests at heart, and to know when, how and why there may be times to radically shift obedience to your own inner authority. True obedience, in its highest form, is the opportunity to practice adherence to and honoring of life-affirming principles and purposes. In your worldly relatings, obedience can mean obeying parents who are concerned with your care and well-being, obeying teachers' instructions for your greater learning, obeying rules and laws that govern safety for all, obeying agreements, contracts and rules of the workplace, obeying emotional and spiritual commitments, and so on. These are all voluntary, involving your willingness, and giving you a sense of belonging and a way to learn, grow, interact cooperatively and have a sense of belonging. To disobey is to rebel against a request, command, rule or status quo in favor of a different preference or an inner calling for something else – even if you don't yet know what that is.

In obeying something inside yourself, you often venture into both inner and outer unknowns, the different and the new – things which may bring challenges, even hurt – but also potentially the greatest joys of self-discovery and purpose. Some of the great achievements by humankind have come from those who, in obeying their own instincts and intuitions, disobeyed what was already known, usual, demanded or expected of them. Disobedience that is motivated by the higher principles of love and truth sooner or later show life-affirming results. And here we say 'sooner or later,' because when an order is disturbed by disobedience, at first there may be disruption, chaos, upset, and so on. On a personal level, loved ones may feel angry, hurt or confused, and you may even feel ashamed or guilty. However, your barometer for whether obedience or disobedience is the right thing is to know if it's the true thing – and if your ultimate goal is to create or destroy, even though the status quo may be disrupted at first.

Thus may my light as LEHAHIAH help you see whether it is obedience or disobedience that is true and life-affirming for you – and if you are willing to bear the consequences. When obedience in a relationship consistently quashes your own individuation, or when disobedience to 'authorities' around you land you out on your own without certain relationships, home or work – then set about preparing a new place and way for yourself where you are, or if necessary, elsewhere. And if you have to wait a bit to obey your inner authority, be patient. Hold your truth in your heart until you can carry it into action in your world. For ultimately your own heart is your greatest ally, and those in your life who respect that will be your truest friends and loved ones. Amen...

4/25 * 7/9 * 9/21pm + 22 * **12/3** * 2/11

35 CHAVAKIAH

(cha-VA-kee-YAH)
Reconciliation (R)
'One who resolves paradox'
Archangel ~ CHAMAEL
Virgo / Jupiter (9/13-17)

I AM THAT WHICH...

helps to use divisiveness as a way to recognize individualities and to transform communication through listening, empathy and the willingness to consider solutions that allow everyone to get what they need. When you are at odds with each other, it is often because each of you view the other's position or goals as opposing your own. There can be so much concern about one's own interests that no one is listening to what the other wants or feels. Accusation, blame, pride and stubbornness escalate, and the divide gets wider. If you really want to get what you want, then you must be willing to consider what others want as well. In order to discover that, it helps to put aside your assumptions about what they want and listen to not only what they say, but what they mean. Sometimes you or the other may know what you want, but don't realize there may be a different way to get it than what you are fixed on. Reconciliation is possible when you negotiate the 'how' rather than arguing about the 'what.' This approach works with intimate relationships just as much as with colleagues and contract negotiations, and what you get is the same – the possibility to continue or leave a situation without harboring ongoing rancor and resentment which can poison subsequent relatings in the same situation or overflow into dynamics with others.

Divisiveness among family members can degenerate a family legacy for generations to come until someone has love enough to stop the 'pain-chain' of blame and extend the forgiveness and compassion which brings reconciliation and new life. The only bounty you can leave behind and still take with you at every leaving is love. Whether you are walking out of the room or out of this lifetime, the connecting threads and lifelines of love and togetherness become the vibrational fabric from which new beginnings and subsequent generations are engendered. Yes, family dynamics can be deeply difficult, but they are also the potential locus of your most profound healing.

I invite you to draw from my CHAVAKIAH light of reconciliation to realize that if the cost of getting what one wants is to disenfranchise another, then the 'win' is illusory. On the spirit level, you are all one, cut from the same eternal cloth into different forms to give you time and space to magnify your own unique colors in order to create a more magnificent tapestry of the whole. Listen to each other, learn from and create with each other, and remember that it is never too late to re-approach from the higher heart-ground of empathy and compassion. For only with these may hearts be reconciled and differences dissolved in acceptance, appreciation and renewal. Amen...

4/26 * 7/10 * 9/23 * **12/4** * 2/12

36 MENADEL

(MEH-na-DEL)
Inner/Outer Work (S)
'One who dances two worlds into one'
Archangel ~ CHAMAEL
Virgo / Mars (9/18-23)

I AM THAT WHICH...

helps you to recognize personality conflicts, long harbored hurts and other difficulties with loved ones, friends or co-workers as reflections of issues that need healing within yourself. Since issues of your own within can be difficult to discern, your outer relatings provide inner mirrors and the means to address what they reflect about yourself. If you have had a longstanding rift with someone, explore the nature of it and look for its seeds and shadows within you. For example, if their hurt against you was betrayal, in what ways have you betrayed yourself? Or perhaps you are being called to re-form your understanding of trust, and to place your trust not in others and their actions and promises, but in your own resiliency and willingness to withstand the vacillations, occasional transgressions and growing pains that are in the nature of all human beingness.

If a partner leaves you, look at how you might have abandoned yourself throughout the relationship. If you feel continually resentful toward someone, what is it they have that you feel you don't or can't get for yourself? If you translate someone sharing information with you as an

135

implication that you're ignorant, and that they are a 'know-it-all,' look at what may be your own feelings of inferiority and self-judgment, and the fear of others perceiving you the way you perceive yourself. If you take offense at others speaking of their successes, rather than admiring and learning from them, what have you not accomplished in your own life that is still disturbing to you?

You will always perceive the actions and attitudes of others toward you through the filter of your own self-perceptions, and you will take personally anything that triggers judgments you already hold against yourself. All 'shadow' issues can divide and weaken you individually and in context with others. That said, any reactive 'negative' eruption, especially triggering a longstanding grudge, is an opportunity for awareness and healing. A family member, intimate or colleague who rubs you the wrong way is like a grain of sand in the 'oyster' of your life which can ultimately yield a shining pearl of wisdom and transformation!

And so, dear inner-outer excavator and explorer, I offer my light-services within you to illuminate the real issues between you and another by focusing on what is being triggered in you rather than what is wrong with the other person. With my steady ever-presence, cultivate the habit of seeing every difficult or uncomfortable issue in your relatings and relationships as gifts of opportunity to work out your personal 'stuff.' In this way, your 'enemies' will become your allies, those who hurt you will show where you need healing, and those who do not appreciate you will inspire you to appreciate yourself. When you take everyone and every happening into your heart, there is nothing that love cannot transform. Amen...

4/27 * 7/11 * 9/24 * **12/5** * 2/13

37 ANIEL

(AH-nee-EL)
Breaking the Circle (G)
'One who lifts you out of the circle into the light'
Archangel ~ CHAMAEL
Libra / Sun (9/24-28)

I AM THAT WHICH...

helps you to break out of stagnant attitudes and long-harbored emotional injuries in order to rehabilitate the past and create a new atmosphere of love, light and harmony in your relatings. You have a saying that 'you can't keep doing the same thing and expect different results.' What you may call a cycle of bad luck in relationships is simply a repetition of the same behavior and choices that keep having the same outcome. You are the only common denominator in relationships or work scenarios that don't work out again and again. Believe it or not, life is always on your side – even when you're not. If you keep ending up in the same place it's because you are taking the same route every time. If you find yourself in the same argument over and over with your partner or a family member, it is because both of you have fallen into the habit of relating in the same way, reacting to the same triggers, and becoming angry with each other for doing 'the same old thing' or going down the same road yet again. In order to end up in a different place, there must be a willingness by at least one person to change the approach.

If you dread holidays and times of family gathering, it is likely because you dread the same undermining dynamics – being seen in the same old way and not being acknowledged and appreciated for the person you are now. Sometimes family members need to see you in the same way because they are secretly ashamed of their own 'same old' lives – as in the 'misery loves company' paradigm. But you can begin to change these dynamics by not reacting in your same old way. Have a different conversation. Ask a question and listen for the answer. Show appreciation for something about them. Relinquish what you already think you know for learning something new. Don't let your resentment be 'the tail that wags your dog' every time the other barks at you. You don't have to react the same way to the same scenario. That's the control you have in every situation, every conversation and encounter. The key is to become conscious of where you would rather get to and keep your eye on that while your heart is changing up the journey!

And so dear one, I offer you my light as ANIEL to help you re-approach in order to help create a more mutually loving and respectful way of relating, no matter what your differences with others. In every case, if you start from the heart, and stay in your heart wherever the dynamics take you, then you will surely arrive somewhere new and better – even in the heart of the other. With mutual forgiveness, compassion and understanding, the circle will no longer be a black hole of impossibility, but a whole in which something life-affirming is possible between you as you realize that at the heart, what you both, and all, truly want is to feel loved. Amen...

4/28 * 7/12 * 9/25 * **12/6** * 2/14

38 HAAMIAH

(ha-AH-mee-YAH)
Ritual and Ceremony (G)
'One who enlivens the path with love'
Archangel ~ CHAMAEL
Libra / Venus (9/29-10/3)

I AM THAT WHICH...

helps you to use gathering times with family and friends to celebrate love and togetherness and to practice the caring, compassion and kindness which is central to any life-affirming belief, ritual or practice. Ritual and ceremony is a way in which you renew and celebrate the milestones and meanings in your lives with each other. Your birth rituals, spiritual and life passages and commemorations, holy days and holidays, graduations, weddings, birthdays, funerals, and so on, are all opportunities to remember and show appreciation for what matters in your lives together. And in all your relatings, relationships and gatherings, nothing matters more than love. Remember this when you argue over wedding decorations or whose house you will go to for a holiday dinner or what religion a child should be brought up in. Remember love when you come together at a church, synagogue, temple, mosque or any holy shrine – whether of your own creed or not. Remember love when someone does not share your belief or way of expressing it. Remember love when all your constructs fail, because sooner or later they will.

All things and people in life come and go as the tides of life ebb and flow. It is the natural ritual of life to express and expend itself in order to renew itself again and again. And with all that passes, the only thing that remains, truly, is love and the truths that love continues to reveal which make their mark in the generations of humankind. And while your keepsakes, treasure boxes and memory books are all essentially for remembering and revisiting particular moments of love, those gatherings and rituals are now in the past, while the love itself lives on in the eternity of your heart. But without love among you, memories and meanings are lost, and ritual loses the vibrancy of an ever-evolving truth to become an empty husk of obligation and conformity. Love is the 'inner' in all your outer devotionals and practices – the humility that bends your knees in prayer, the commitment that sits you down in the stillness of meditation, the willingness that joins gathered hearts to magnify the presence of the Divine within and among you.

And so my HAAMIAH light-purpose dear loved and loving one is to amplify the love and light in your gathering times, and to help you reinvigorate your rituals and ceremonies when meaning has become stale and forgotten. Remember love also in your smallest daily rituals – picking up your clothes or cleaning up after yourself so that your spouse or parent or roommate doesn't have to...asking each other how you are...smiling in welcome to each other...using kindness and care in how you treat those you share your life with. And let part of your practice be to greet the strangers around you who are 'friends you just don't know yet.' Be willing to learn about each other's rituals and discover that the sameness in your differences always waits in your hearts for recognition and a shared sense of belonging. Amen...

4/29 * 7/13 * 9/26 * **12/7** * 2/15

39 REHAEL

(RAY-ha-EL)
Filial Submission (G)
'One who honors what was while inspiring what will be'
Archangel ~ CHAMAEL
Libra / Mercury (10/4-8)

I AM THAT WHICH...

helps to create love-and-life affirming relationships among parents and children, so that a positive heritage of family essence, values and integrity may be honored even while new generations carry forward renewed vitality through their own variations and creations. The deeper importance in the humanistic and spiritual ethics of 'honor thy mother and father' is to clear the generations of harbored hurts and resentments so that what may be carried forward are the legacies of love and truth that help each and all to fulfill your own true purposes for being.

Honoring those who came before you can be very challenging if they seemed to be negligent, cruel or unloving. As children you submit to your parents, even with their seeming mistakes and 'bad' acts, because you need the safety of knowing they are there. Ultimately, in the subtleties of 'filial submission,' it is important to understand that what you essentially submitted to was the teaching you received from them. Thereby you honor their contribution, as well as the greaterness of your own life, by your willingness to choose differently because of their example. This is the way the true warrior honors and respects his 'enemy' as his greatest ally – by sharpening his own strength on the other's sword. In your willingness to heal and change the potential negative effect of the past by going forward in your own life in a more loving way, you also keep the actions of those who came before from contaminating the generations after you.

In the opposite scenario, where the parents are loving and well-intentioned, children may rebel and behave as if their familial influences are quite terrible! These things are often underlying matters of the soul that are not discernible in 'cause-and-effect' terms. Or a son or daughter may simply want to live a very different life than what parents may have encouraged and provided the means to. This is most common in the parents' desire for their child to pursue a particular course of study or career, when the child's desire and interests are in another field, or still being explored. True filial submission does not call for the child to fulfill the parent's choice of career or lifestyle – but rather to 'submit' to the inner authority that propels individuation. Thus the child's passage into adulthood comes by asserting his or her own true calling, which is the true fulfillment of the parent's underlying desire for the child's happiness and well-being.

Thus, dear parents and children, draw on my light as REHAEL to cherish each other's contributions and individualities. For everything you become affects those who came before you and those who will come after you. And know that the legacies you carry forth and those you newly create will be loving, true and utterly unique if they have proceeded from the inner authority of your own heart. Amen...

4/30 * 7/14 * 9/27 * **12/8** * 2/16

40 YEIAZEL

(YAY-ah-ZEL)
Divine Consolation and Comfort (G)
'One who is a soft landing for your heart'
Archangel ~ CHAMAEL
Libra / Moon (10/9-13)

I AM THAT WHICH...

helps you to bring to each other the comfort of unconditional love, acceptance, compassion that is conveyed through presence and attentive listening. One of the kindest things you can do for each other is to listen. And the kind of listening we mean is that which hears not only what is said, but what longs to be said – that which hears not only the words, but feels the feelings and sees what is not yet visible. In your listenings to each other, do you allow the spaces of silence? Are you thinking of something else, waiting for what you want to hear or for the other to stop talking so that you can speak? Being fully present to another's need for comfort or to share a confidence is both a gift and an opportunity for extraordinary meeting – even if initially it is not easy. If your own within is confused or painful, the unknown of the other's inner can be even more frightening, as if it may 'rub off,' dredge up or compound your own 'inner demons.' Or you may feel too busy or distracted or 'have enough of your own problems' to take in theirs – and thus, you might reply with something 'similar' in your own life that you hope will show commiseration. But the listening that heals is that

143

which receives and sits with the other's feelings in presence and non-judgment, and does not search for sameness between you but honors the other's need and individuality.

When you are heartfully present with another in this way, the way and words you offer come from the wisdom of the eternal and the Divine-in-attendance that knows utterly the heart and soul of the person and the comfort needed in that moment. This shared light-quality of attentive presence for one timeless moment can do more than a thousand casual conversations to inspire the unlimited resources of one's own within to awaken. In that one wondrous moment 'where two are gathered,' burdens are lightened and strength renewed.

Thus do I give you my loving comfort-light as YEIAZEL so that you might come to see how you can be each other's soft landings. Your hearts have an infinite resiliency for cushioning life's many challenges, and your 'wrap-around' arms have an invisible wingspan that lifts and protects. And indeed, with love and presence, you likely won't need to go down the other's dark 'rabbit hole!' For love is the great dark-dissolver! Bring it on and the dark will begin to dissolve the way any dark does when the light appears. Thus, dear one, be not afraid of each other's moment of need or pain – for every moment you tend to another, you are being tended also by the Angels and all that is Divine. So just love and listen and love some more. That is all. Literally, that is All. Amen...

December 9 – 16

Angels 41 – 48

Sephira 6

TIPHARETH ~ Beauty, Harmony

Overlighting Archangel

MIKHAEL ~ 'Who is as God'
(Governs with RAPHAEL*) Power and will;
ignites strength, courage and protection for
spiritual seeking and healing

41 HAHAHEL
42 MIKAEL
43 VEULIAH
44 YELAHIAH
45 SEALIAH
46 ARIEL
47 ASALIAH
48 MIHAEL

* Note that the Archangel correspondences in Sephirot 6 and 8 have been interchanged throughout the centuries by different Kabbalists and schools of thought. After additional research which shows the ways in which both Archangels are active in both Sephirot, the primary Archangel correspondences presented in the original *Birth Angels* book are reversed here, but each are included as co-governing.

41 HAHAHEL

(HAH-hah-HEL)
Mission (R)
'One who brings Heaven to Earth'
Archangel ~ MIKHAEL (with RAPHAEL)
Libra / Uranus (10/14-18)

I AM THAT WHICH...

helps you to 'prepare a place' in your hearts for the higher ground of Spirit between and among you, and to use the expression of your soul purposes as your service to and with others for the expansion of love and truth in all that you are individually and together. Whether the details of your mission call you to being of service to others professionally or personally, 'holding space' in your relatings for the fullness of Spirit to be in attendance instills in your hearts a 'Way' to meet the challenges of your individualities and togetherness with understanding and healing. The Divine Spirit is composed of the fluidities of Love and Truth, and allowing it to be the 'third' between you and another turns the improbable to the possible, a falling down to standing back up, distance into closeness, trials into triumphs, separation into unity. Having faith in the infinite and diverse ways of Love reveals and increases the truths within and between you. And whether your truths bind you together or let you go, you will be empowered and buoyed by the greaterness of this Love that knows utterly who you are and will always watch over you from within.

The mission of all beings is to fulfill the purposes of your souls in cooperation with the emotional, mental and physical parts of your humanity. While each person's journey of individuation is to advance from karma to dharma – from healing to helping – your respective 'mission details' as to how, where and why is unique to the expression of your personal love and truth in what you are called to do. What may seem to be a sacrifice from the perspective of onlookers may be a self-fulfillment for the do-er. A trip around the corner for one is a pathway to the cosmos for another. What is monumental or miraculous to some is 'all in a day's work' for others. No one's purpose is more or less important than another's, and those who realize this acknowledge everyone's contribution with respect. And you do not have to be totally healed to help another, nor must you have arrived at a destination to point the way to a fellow traveler. It is having the humility and compassion to be companions to each other on the road that is often the greatest service. The more you help, the more you can heal, and the more you teach, the more you can learn. As you evolve, your service to others does not deplete you, but rather fulfills you.

So dear mission-and-purpose-seeking one, please do draw from my HAHAHEL light to see that at the heart of all missions is to love yourselves and each other. In first loving yourself as you are loved by the Divine, you may know how to love others truly and rightly. For love is the 'prime mover' of truth – the I Am that is the totality of the Divine – which is inherent in the isness of you and him and her and every being. Individually and together, you root the Divine on Earth through the true fulfillment of your beings – and in the presence of love, you cannot help but increase and deepen in truth. Amen...

5/2 * 7/16 * 9/29 * **12/10** * 2/18

42 MIKAEL

(MIH-kah-EL)
Political Authority and Order (R)
'One who helps you find your guiding light'
Archangel ~ MIKHAEL (with RAPHAEL)
Libra / Saturn (10/19-23)

I AM THAT WHICH...

helps to encourage and maintain heart-centric dynamics among you and your loved ones, friends and close associates so that love, compassion, forgiveness and mutual fulfillment are the guiding principles of your interactions. Imagine if there would be an ongoing agreement within your intimate circles that all concerns, issues and disagreements would be brought before the soft authorities of the heart, with the intention to respect the needs and desires of each and all? Gone would be rigidity, suppression of feelings, resentment and other fear-based ways of interacting that can stifle and derail closeness. Instead, love and truth would govern, with the receptivity and openness that sees and appreciates who each is. The same fluidity and flexibility which encourages the growth of individuals would also contribute to the richness of your relationships. You would enjoy a quality of togetherness that is able to incorporate diverse perspectives and what matters most to each individual. Thus, each might pursue your unique purposes without drawing lines that cannot be crossed or having to leave each other behind in order to grow further.

In many cases, it is the stifling of individuality that takes the vitality out of relationship. The healthiest partnerships, families and groups are those in which individuation and commitment to togetherness are mutually conducive. No one's dream or beingness is suppressed or 'sacrificed' for another's – but rather the whole organizes itself around the needs of all its members, so that desires and fulfillments of each are more about when and how than if or if not.

Thus, may you use my MIKAEL light to help you cultivate your collective hearts – and the personal truths, wisdoms, intuitions and feelings of love and compassion contained therein – to be the authority in your relationships. Be vulnerable and receptive as you listen to each other's within, and let your expectations be that your relationships will encourage and welcome individual growth. By so doing, each of you will be more able to keep your own inner wells full, so that you can drink from each other's hearts without any being drained or parched. In this way, as you thrive as individuals, the thriving will permeate your relationships so that they become more vital and whole. Thereby you may be the support, launch pad and soft landing each can count on for encouragement, fulfillment, comfort and rejuvenation – again and again. Amen...

5/3 * 7/17 * 9/30 * **12/11** * 2/19

43 VEULIAH

(vay-OO-lee-AH)
Prosperity (R)
'One who shines the light of possibility'
Archangel ~ MIKHAEL (with RAPHAEL)
Scorpio / Jupiter (10/24-28)

I AM THAT WHICH...

helps you to appreciate and magnify the heart-wealth of family, friendship and community in cooperation, encouragement, generosity and gratitude. Wealth of any kind is essentially a 'cache' of accumulated energy. Prosperity, however, is the ongoing flow and exchange of life-affirming energy between and among you. While you most often relate these words and concepts to money and other forms of barter, there is no energy more powerful and abundant than the creation energy of love – and none more readily available. No matter what your material circumstances may be, love is always present, accessible and instantly increasable by your awareness of it and your willingness to allow its flow to move toward you and through you unto others. With the flow of love, all other prosperities become available to you if you so desire and direct the flow of your love to include those areas. Because money is energy, it is not wrong to love money, and loving it can draw it to you. It is when you hoard what comes to you without allowing the flow of exchange to continue, that love degrades into fear and ultimately poverty of spirit.

As adults, you have likely forgotten about particular trinkets or 'toys' you wanted that your parents did or did not buy you – but you probably remember what you were or were not given that money could not buy. The most important gift you can give to your children and each other is love, for love has an unlimited power to empower and bring to each what is needed and desired. Many times people give money when they don't know how to give of themselves. That said, people give what they can give, and what is most readily available to them, and that is fair and noble still. However, the gift of self – your talent, your time, your presence in listening and comforting – is a gift that keeps on giving, even after you've 'left the building.' Thus, dear one let your monetary generosities be accompanied by a personal expression of caring, a follow-up on how someone is doing, a word or letter of encouragement – for such kindness will resonate immeasurably and be remembered far longer than the dollar amount you gave.

My VEULIAH light is within you to help amplify the energy of love so that you may be bountiful and prosperous at your foundation. May there be love for yourself and the Divine within you, love of your work and love of others in your intimate and community circles, including love of the Earth which physically sustains you. Thus your life and your legacy will yield that which cannot be counted nor ended, but rather taken in and passed on from one heart to another forever and ever. Amen...

5/4 * 7/18 * 10/1 * **12/12** * 2/20

44 YELAHIAH

(yay-LA-hee-YAH)
Karmic Warrior (R)
'One who heals the past by loving it.'
Archangel ~ MIKHAEL (with RAPHAEL)
Scorpio / Mars (10/29-11/2)

I AM THAT WHICH...

helps you to understand the eruption of issues between you and another as hurt coming to the surface to be healed. The 'karmic battles' of healing are engaged not only for you and those close to you, but also for your entire generation and those before and after you. 'Karma' is not about punishment for past 'mistakes' or 'wrongs,' but the opportunity to make different choices in order to restore equilibrium and equanimity. Healing dissolves life-negating energies that have been harbored within your soul since anywhere from a minute to eons ago. Those who are closest to you play a part in your healing as they are simultaneously working on issues with you to heal themselves.

To be a karmic warrior for healing is about winning a battle that cannot be fought. When an issue emerges between you and another, reactivity and resistance indicates that there is more to the issue than may be initially evident. If you let aggravation and argument lead you to real and depthful communication, you may get underneath the reactive surface to unearth and ultimately heal whatever wounds are there.

Pain, anger, fear, pride, jealousy, resentment and all seemingly negative emotional experiences that can happen with others are alerts and opportunities for healing. If you follow the often tangled threads of your emotions, you may find the original 'knot' that began the strangling of your heart and tied off the circulation of some of your vital energies. If you are willing to do battle with, instead of against, each other, then your 'enemy' can become your ally and the healing you win together will be more than either of you could have won on your own. For this, you will need to make your way to your own heart, and then the other's. In doing so, you will enable more than the two of you to be healed, more than you can imagine, seen and unseen.

And so, dear heart-seeking warrior, I offer you my light as YELAHIAH to call up between you and another in moments of emotional trial. This light cannot be used as a sword or shield, but as an illumination sharp and true that pierces your hearts through and through unto the surrender of love and the sacred co-creation of 'duel' healing. So advance dear hearts, one to another, wielding your inner Divine light, as you prepare to die to the old and be reborn anew together unto love and the release of a new and healing truth. Amen...

5/5 * 7/19 * 10/2 * **12/13** * 2/21

45 SEALIAH

(say-A-Lee-YAH)
Motivation and Willfulness (S)
'One who fires your heart-motor'
Archangel ~ MIKHAEL (with RAPHAEL)
Scorpio / Sun (11/3-7)

I AM THAT WHICH...

helps you to purify your motivations and use your will rightly and respectfully in your relatings with others so that the true desires, purposes and choosings of each should not be eclipsed by any other, but rather supported and encouraged. Just as the choosings of your own will are respected by your Divine soul-parentage, Angelic allies and numerous unseen guardians and helpers, so may you extend that same respect to your loved ones, friends and peers of all kinds. When your motivations toward each other are rooted in a genuine appreciation and desire for the fulfillment of the other's own aspirations and choices, then you add to the energetic support each of you needs to help cultivate and succeed in your unique purposes. It may be relatively easy to support the choices of your friends and associates without emotional investment in their choosings. With relatives and other loved ones, however, it is often a different story. Your most pure emotional interest is for those you love to do well so that they might be happy and successful. While at times you may recognize before they do what their special gifts and talents are, if you try to prescribe or insist upon what they should do, or what you want, or even demand them to do – then it is your happiness you are pursuing – not theirs.

If you have ever had your own will as it pertains to your sense of purpose overridden by another – whether a parent, sibling, partner or 'corporate ladder' – then you know the sense of frustration, out-of-syncness, emptiness and perhaps even anger or shame at going along with it. Such is the scenario when a parent puts a child through school on the condition that it be the school and course of study that the parent wants, or when one person's work or interests repeatedly override their partner's – or when your own sense of professional 'shoulds' keep you tethered to unsatisfying jobs with remuneration and responsibilities that seem too great to walk away from.

Your purpose and reason for being can only be amply fed by the fire in your own belly, the truth in your own heart, the destiny held in your own soul. And no matter your relationship, no one's will is more or less important than another's, whatever the motivations and choices. And so my SEALIAH light says unto each of you, give others roots in your love and allow their own inner Divine to give them wings. Thus may each find their own star in the waiting sky, the one that belongs to them and their dreams and none other. And let there be the kind of prospering that each chooses, in your own way and time, for your own right and reason. Amen...

5/6 * 7/20 * 10/3 * **12/14** * 2/22

46 ARIEL

(AH-ree-EL)
Perceiver and Revealer (G)
'One who demystifies the mysteries'
Archangel ~ MIKHAEL (with RAPHAEL)
Scorpio / Venus (11/8-12)

I AM THAT WHICH...

helps you to cultivate intuitive perception of people and motivations through the inner guidance of love and truth; thus may you see the unseen, hear the unsaid and reveal the innermost loves, truths, longings and possibilities within the hearts and souls of others. If you have the gift of seeing what is not always visible, you must realize that no matter how much you may seem to see, you will not see the whole truth of another unless you are looking through the eyes of your heart. For it is love that brings forth and reveals the deeper mysteries of each other in any relating or relationship. And that mystery is about the more of each of you that longs to be felt, known and perceived – and that in being so seen by the other can make it so.

Has there been someone in at least one moment of your life who you felt truly saw you? A seeing so loving and true that it eclipsed your self-judgment and parted the veil of your partial self-perceptions to give you a glimpse of your magnificent potential? Have you done this for another and felt the humbling gratitude at being a conduit for that light? This is how the Divine sees you always, and this is the holy seeing that you can offer to each other through the Divine Light you carry in your hearts and souls.

The opportunity of anyone in your life who does not see the sacred light of your isness, either in expression or potential, is to make you willing to see yourself. You do not ever have to believe that what another does not see about you does not exist. Just as some people cannot see reds or greens or other colors, some will not be able to see your own wondrous hues. That may be their loss, but it should not be yours. For what they don't see says more about them than you. True love is not blind, but rather all-seeing, seeing both what is here and what is still on the way. Those who have love enough can be a true see-er of others. And only with love should what is seen be revealed. For in the power of true-seeing, potential is released and purpose is quickened.

Thus, dear one, use my ARIEL light to be seer and sayer of what only love and truth may see and tell. May the gaze of your seeing quicken the soul-memories of others, as the words of your telling bring the light of possibility to their hearts. May you have the joy of this for the sake of their joy and for the sake of the Divine that dwells within you, acting as you in these most sacred moments for their benefit. Thus may you be a conduit for love's creation energy to flow forth as a river of life wherein another's truth of being may be anointed. Amen...

5/7 * 7/21 * 10/4 * **12/15** * 2/23

47 ASALIAH

(ah-SA-lee-YAH)
Contemplation (G)
'One who sees the patterns and purposes'
Archangel ~ MIKHAEL (with RAPHAEL)
Scorpio / Mercury (11/13-17)

I AM THAT WHICH...

helps you to call forth in each other the sacred 'temple-gifts' of the Divine imprinted within your souls so that you might come into fullness on Earth as a Divine-Human being. Each person's Divine-origined soul holds a template, a kind of cosmic blueprint, of that part of the Divine 'image and likeness' you embody, which has endowed you with certain qualities to be cultivated, purposed and shared with others. This soul-template is broadcast to your heart, which becomes the locus of your personal truth and all that you love and are urged to purpose. The opportunity of 'contemplation' is that through stillness, prayer, meditation, creativity, being in nature or in the simple joy of true meeting between you and another, this 'holy temple' becomes awakened within you.

In 'the peace that surpasses all understanding,' you may come to know the nature of the Heavens at play within the nature of your own unique love and purpose on Earth. In true-seeing presence with another, you become wise and intuitive mirrors and catalysts for each other and the particularities of the Divine within you. In quickening and

159

witnessing the holy within each other, your soul purposes and potentials are inspired and revealed as you root the Heavens upon Earth. And 'where two or more are gathered, there shall I be,' the making of two is so much more than one plus one.

Great are the moments for both the Divine and the Human when you perceive and express your inner temples in beingness and co-creation with others. To kneel with another at the altar of two-hearts-as-one – whether as partners, friends, family or seeming strangers – is to know and feel the grace of Divine Love that is your eternal nature and which powers and purposes your time and beingness on Earth as an individual and in togetherness with others. In the sacredness of your shared inner temples, you come to know the Truth that there is no end to this great Love, only its never-ending expansion that prevails sooner or later within all – even in those who have forgotten you were born of Love, for there is nothing or no one who is not.

And so my temple light as ASALIAH is given unto you that we of the Divine might draw you into the temple of your heart and let it be from here that you give yourself in presence and gathering with others. And know that all the Angels shall be in attendance hereby. For as your holy books say in different ways, whatever happens in the inner temple of the heart and between one heart and another is felt and known both in the heavens and on Earth. In such moments all the universes rejoice in the beauties and harmonies of co-creation and the never-ending energies of Love and Truth that compose and quicken you for the sake of your loving and true selves, each other and the expression of the Divine on Earth. Amen...

5/8 * 7/22 * 10/5 * **12/16** * 2/24

48 MIHAEL

(MIH-a-EL)
Fertility and Fruitfulness (G)
'One who taps the light-elixirs of life'
Archangel ~ MIKHAEL (with RAPHAEL)
Scorpio / Moon (11/18-22)

I AM THAT WHICH...

helps to foster conjugal, familial and collaborative vibrancy in which individual potentials are fulfilled, and relationship and co-creativity are continually renewed through the unique contributions and vitalities of each person. In romantic partnerships and committed relationships, there is a coming together as a 'unit' – which may naturally inspire you to put aside some things for the sake of 'the relationship.' At the same time your intimate relatings and sense of being allies will have ongoing joy and fruitfulness if you also allow each other to be who you truly are and continue to aspire toward the dreams and goals of your individualities as well as for your partnership. We suggest a partnering that is as a 'pas de deux' of individuation and togetherness in which the melodies of flexibility, fluidity and interdependence are continually playing! As you go toward and away, toward and away, you each gather diversity of experience to bring back into the relationship to enrich the oneness.

Encouraging each other to blossom and shine as individuals will make your togetherness that much stronger and more interesting, vibrant and co-creative. And thus

161

there will be 'love enough to go around' if there are children and extended family and friends, as you enfold them into the remarkable vitality that is possible 'when two are the one that is more than two.'

Much of this holds true in relatings with friendships and colleagues as well, though it can be easier with friends and peers to not feel threatened by the expression of each other's individualities, talents and skills – and to make important life choices without necessarily consulting the other. People must be and are always growing and evolving, no matter how 'unevolved' some may seem at times. As with relatings of any kind that are long-lived, sustaining interest in each other without ever thinking you know everything there is to know about the other will create a vibrant atmosphere where mutual discovery rather than assumptions thrive! And just as with colleagues who are collaborating on a project or business together, 'wherever two or more are gathered' in co-creativity, the creation energy of love abides, and truths both personal and joint are expanded and evolved.

And so I joyfully lend you my light as MIHAEL to commingle with and amplify yours in all your relatings, that you may revel and shine in fertility and fruitfulness individually and together. For ultimately the blossoms of individuality in the context of togetherness will have more petals, more hues, more aromatic potency than if each were standing in a field alone. Thus, because of togetherness, the fruit of each shall be juicier with more savor – and because of each other, so shall your togetherness. Amen...

December 17 – 24

Angels 49 – 56

Sephira 7

NETZACH ~ Victory

Overlighting Archangel

HANIEL ~ 'Grace of God'
Joy, light, insight and true unselfish love
through relationship with the Divine

---

49 VEHUEL

50 DANIEL

51 HAHASIAH

52 IMAMIAH

53 NANAEL

54 NITHAEL

55 MEBAHIAH

56 POYEL

5/9 * 7/23 * 10/6 * **12/17** * 2/25

49 VEHUEL

(VAY-hoo-EL)
Elevation, Grandeur (R)
'One who in-spirits the magnificence of the higher'
Archangel ~ HANIEL
Sagittarius / Uranus (11/23-27)

I AM THAT WHICH...

helps you to take the higher roads of love, compassion, generosity and forgiveness in your relatings, thereby inspiring others to do the same and elevating your shared consciousness and interactions to 'something more.' Many of you wish you could elevate the quality of relatings with your relations, since families are often 'hotbeds' for escalating reactions over old issues. Some of the things that trigger 'the same old thing' is failing to see or look for newness in each other, making assumptions based on long-held judgments, and continuing to blame and punish and harbor old hurts. But all of these things can begin to be lifted up out of their stale, swampy mire by taking a step up to the higher ground of heart. As we often say, in every issue, challenge or long-harbored hurt, all it takes is one willing heart to begin to turn the tide of resentment, anger, stubbornness and pride. One person who declines to react to a potentially inflammatory situation can keep negative emotions from recycling, and open up new lines of communication for greater mutual understanding.

Though you may sometimes bring each other down, your power to lift each other up is infinite. 'All you need is love,' as your wise ones have simply said. For with love comes all the resources of heart and soul – compassion, forgiveness, wisdom, insight and understanding. And with love comes access to the eternal within the present that can ennoble any kind of moment between you and another and enable you to discover a more whole truth together.

You can begin by expressing gratitude for what was and is good between you. And by acknowledging your part, without excuses or justifications. By asking questions, without blame or accusation. By listening, without interruption or taking exception. With love you may know the truth beyond any perceived hurt or wrong-doing – which is that each soul manifested on Earth is in collaboration with other souls to dissolve impedances to the flow of love. Thereby the truth of each may be expressed and the Divine within you may be more deeply rooted on Earth through your elevated and ennobled human beingness.

You are all playing roles for each other which your souls have agreed to, and as your consciousness is raised by love you will begin to remember these soul-truths that hold the answers to all your questions, confusions, longings and hopes with each other. Thus may my VEHUEL light help you to take the higher road of the heart in your relatings, and to remind you where it is when you have forgotten. Only this higher ground can give you a vista above and beyond the 'low-ceilinged sky' of pain and reaction, the possibility for a new dawning of light between you, and a new way of being with and within each other. Amen...

5/10 * 7/24 * 10/7 * **12/18** * 2/26

50 DANIEL

(DAH-nee-EL)
Eloquence (R)
'One who uses words to bring forth life'
Archangel ~ HANIEL
Sagittarius / Saturn (11/28-12/2)

I AM THAT WHICH...

helps you to be mindful to let your thoughts pass through your heart before they leave your lips. Words can be waymakers or weapons, having the power to unify or divide, reconcile or polarize, bring you together with others or tear you asunder. Words that pass through your heart before they are unleashed upon the minds and hearts of others are words that have been more nobly fashioned with wisdom, compassion and understanding. Even if you deliver intelligent and remarkable truths unto others, without love they will be only half-truths, and as such can be piercing, defeating and even destructive. On the other hand, words laced with the greater knowing of love illuminate potential and possibility and inspire new life where there might have been dullness, doubt and fear before.

People use words for all sorts of reasons, self-expression being chief among them – but in communication with others you must also consider what kind of energy, atmosphere and possibility you want to create between you. If you are speaking to be heard by the other – not just to fill the silence or hear yourself talk – then you must speak in a language

167

the other can understand. And it may not be your 'native' language – for that person may be from a 'different tribe' with different orientations and reference points. But rather than thinking you have to 'tone yourself down' or suppress who you are – because that steals your own vibrancy – instead 'translate yourself' into a language they can hear. It's what your parents did for you when you were a child, and it may be what you ultimately must do for them as an adult in a world that is different from the one they grew you up in. You may not want to speak in the language of their past or their habitual reference points – but there is no more universal language than love. Speaking from the feeling-language of the heart stirs heart. For whatever you intend to convey, what wants to be heard is love and possibility.

The secret power of words, whether spoken or written, is that in their ability to create or destroy, they actually transmit those energies to those who receive them. So, dear word-wielder of power, use my light as DANIEL to choose your words lovingly with children, partners, and other family and loved ones – for they hear you in a way they hear no one else for as long as they shall live. Thus, let your words that play over and over in their heads be those from your heart – words that inspire and encourage, that accept and forgive, and which let them know and feel that you will always love them no matter what. And when more difficult words must be spoken at times, that context of love will thus be a softening as you affirm the other's beingness, even while declaring your own, so that there will be possibility for each of you and also between you. The first word spoken in the universe was light and created light, including ultimately the soul-lights of each and all. So dear light-birthed one, in all you say and convey, let there be light. Amen...

5/11 * 7/25 + 26am * 10/8 * **12/19** * 2/27

51 HAHASIAH

(ha-HAH-see-YAH)
Universal Medicine (R)
'One who draws from the Oneness to heal'
Archangel ~ HANIEL
Sagittarius / Jupiter (12/3-7)

I AM THAT WHICH...

brings the universal remedy of Oneness-memory to extract the divisive "worm in the apple" among difficult relationship dynamics so that healing and closeness can be created or restored. Universal medicine in the realm of emotions and relationship is composed of any thought, feeling, word or act which can heal the hurt of betrayal or unbelonging and the pain of feeling unloved. Often it takes a time of crisis or tragedy to stop focusing on what someone did or didn't give or do, and instead remember their gifts. If you hold on to what is missing with each other, you will miss what has been holding you aloft all along. If you harbor hurt, healing won't have a work-space within you. If you continually live with judgment of self or others, you are sentencing yourselves to life without love's parole.

If you are willing to 'come up for air' out of murky emotional waters of resentment, anger, pride and so forth, you can begin to see each other in a different light. You may come to realize how you have been the shaping sand in each other's oysters. You may have rubbed one another the 'wrong' way for a time, but in just the right way to turn you

169

into pearls of wisdom and beauty, ready to shine – when you stop going on about your abrasive time together in the oyster! In the light of acceptance, you can see each other as distinct beings striving to grow in the midst of life's challenges and responsibilities – and be able to forgive the roles one or the other was 'supposed to' play but perhaps didn't so well – or did perfectly, but was not the role you wanted them to play! Or you may see the gift in the other's example of what you did not want to be, which helped you to choose differently and become who you are now.

Ultimately the cure for all that ails is to remember that at the soul level you are all diverse 'cuts' from the same eternal 'cloth' of Divine Oneness. In the tapestry of Creation are many-colored threads and a multitude of textures, tones and soul-vistas that are not fixed, but fluid, accommodating individual desires, choices and the unique evolving stories of each. Like a grand jigsaw puzzle, every soul is needed to complete the picture of Creation on Earth and throughout the universes.

Thus dear one, when you struggle with separateness in your outer world, may you ingest a light-dose of my HAHASIAH medicine to return to your Oneness on the inside. And yet, do revel in your differences, for because of each of you and your diverse creations and ways of being the Divine can be known, touched and felt. And so we thank you. Amen...

5/12 * 7/26pm + 27 * 10/9 * **12/20** * 2/28 + 29

52 IMAMIAH

(ee-MAH-mee-YAH)
Expiation of Errors (R)
'One who makes whole'
Archangel ~ HANIEL
Sagittarius / Mars (12/8-12)

I AM THAT WHICH...

helps to bring awareness and healing of difficult familial and interpersonal relatings, and to lighten the weight of your past together by changing your interactions in the present. Nothing so quickly lightens the past than letting it go. But when the past is about difficulties involving others – while one may be able to let go, there is the other. And so, there will likely need to be conversation, mutual listening and the willingness to replace old reactions with new actions and old judgments with new perceptions. Ultimately, whatever seeming truth you each may cling to about the other, it is only when you look through the eyes of your heart that you will be able to see each other in the light of a more whole truth – the parts of each of you that only love can see.

Every healing begins with willingness. So first, you must want to heal yourself, and the relationship, and to remember that if you find yourself being pulled into the heat of 'battle.' Ultimately, when you are able to see your own or the other's seeming mistakes or transgressions as opportunities for your respective awareness and growth, then there will no longer be a need to continue in the ways of resentment, anger, shame or what you call 'passive aggression,' in order to punish, humiliate, or whatever else brings a sense of pay-back, retribution or atonement.

In all cases, your own true at-onement comes when transformation takes place in the inner parts of your being. The other's forgiveness of you may take time, but the changes in your own energy and intent will transmit as energetic light-seeds into their being that sooner or later will crack open and begin to disperse light. The way and timing of that is between the other person and his or her own soul and inner divinity, and thus not for you to wait for, prescribe, monitor or judge. It is enough to have your heart and hands full with your own healing and to keep the door to your heart open so that the other may approach when ready.

Thus is my IMAMIAH light given unto you to illuminate where healing is needed within yourself and with the other and to lighten your heaviness of hurt. It is powerful when one person heals, but when two come together with hearts opened to mutual healing – know that all the Angels rejoice for the love of the heavens that you bring to Earth in these moments. For where two or more are gathered in love's willingness, there shall come new life and new light – not only for the two – but for all, seen and unseen. Amen...

5/13 * 7/28 * 10/10 * **12/21** * 3/1

53 NANAEL

(NA-na-EL)
Spiritual Communication (R)
'One who sends and receives from within'
Archangel ~ HANIEL
Sagittarius / Sun (12/13-16)

I AM THAT WHICH...

helps to bring spiritual presence into your relationships so that hearts might be awakened and soul memories stirred, that you may deepen your mutual feelings and increase your meanings and purposes together. It is easy to not see the treasures that are closest when your attention is always pulling you out into the world. In the comfort and familiarity of family and other long-time relationships, you can miss the miracles of possibility that are right before you and between you in the greater depths of your beings. You may spend your lives journeying far and wide questing for something greater, something hidden, something extraordinary – and all the time it is right here in the journey that, without willingness, can be the longest distance of all – between one heart and another.

The 'hero's journey,' the ' 'walk-about,' the journey of life itself – are all outer journeys that enact and stimulate the inner journey, or 'vision quest.' What the heart seeks can only be found in the inner terrains. For the heart seeks self and soul, reason for being, and especially, true connection with others in which love and the deeper questions of life and beingness can be explored and cultivated. Those who stay on the surface of experiences and relatings do not find what they seek – and may go from one to the other never finding it until they come to believe it doesn't exist. For the 'hidden kingdom' of inner treasures, the 'shangri-la' of an extraordinary life, is often visible only as a light in the eyes of someone who has been there. And those who have are those who went looking for it and were willing to see it everywhere and in everyone.

And so dear one, use my light to see that although those closest to you may be your greatest emotional risks, they are also potentially your true gold mines in plumbing the depths within and between you. Being able to be loving, true and depthful with your loved ones will give you a sense of true home in the world, and the courage and confidence to deepen your relatings with others. One real and true conversation or communion is worth a lifetime of casual friends or lovers. One true meeting of the heart is greater than a hundred jovial pats on the back. One timely resonant word is worth more than a thousand chats about the weather, the news or your neighbors doings! And if your loved ones are reticent about having deeper conversations, then there is always the universal language of love – and her 'daughters,' compassion and forgiveness. Much can be communicated in just being present with each other in small ways, and allowing your sameness of heart to be felt. Thus, dear walking-talking words of creation in form and flesh, you are invited to simply love, and let the way and language of it naturally come. Amen...

5/14 * 7/29 * 10/11 * **12/22** * 3/2

54 NITHAEL

(NIT-ha-EL)
Rejuvenation and Eternal Youth (S)
'One who grows the rose of foreverness within'
Archangel ~ HANIEL
Sagittarius / Venus (12/17-21)

I AM THAT WHICH...

inspires the sharing of impassioned thoughts, feelings and ideas, and times of reveling in the love and joy of togetherness which can restore and renew. There are many ways to relax and rejuvenate – meditation, being in nature, vacationing, body treatments, energy work, exercise, eating healthy foods and even just getting a good night's sleep! But you have likely experienced the deepest levels of renewal in togetherness through the expressions of love, intimate or co-creative conversation and sharing your lives, passions and purposes.

Because love is a creation energy, when you share love, not only is more love manifested – but more of you is manifested as well. Love of yourself, each other, your dreams and creations is what unfolds the many-petaled blossom that you are. And through life's seasons of ebb and flow, it is love that scatters your new seeds of becoming and brings you from periods of seeming dormancy, dullness and darkness back out into the light – sporting new colors of yourself unto the world!

175

You have the power, through loving, to help and inspire each other to blossom anew. Every heart needs to be seen and cradled at times by another physical, feeling being. Sometimes all that is needed is a moment of paying attention, listening and being truly and lovingly present with the other to give a burst of renewal. Indeed, meeting each other at the heart and reconnecting with your passions and enthusiasms can 'recharge your batteries' and give you the energy for continuing on.

And so dear beloved one, I offer you my 'age-defying' light as NITHAEL to rejuvenate you not only on the inside of yourself, but to bring the newness waiting to be expressed within you unto others. And if you are someone who lives alone or works on your own much of the time, know that you do not have to wait for the rejuvenation of love and togetherness to be given to you by another. For such seeming lack may be filled instantly by your willingness to give a loving attentive moment to another. In the words of the Divine recorded in your holy books in different ways, 'whatsoever you do for the least of you, you do for me.' Everyone has a feeling of 'least' at some time during their day, their week, their year, their lives – a time when you feel least loved, least present, least possible. Use my NITHAEL light as your own to notice and attend to each other with kindness – that you may each be reminded you are not alone here. Someone has your back – and your heart – in awareness and caring. No matter what you may have ever suffered in your life, it is love that will always renew you and love that will keep you – if not young in years, for that is so briefly consequential – then surely and certainly eternal. Amen...

5/15 * 7/30 * 10/12 * **12/23** * 3/3

55 MEBAHIAH

(may-BA-hee-YAH)
Intellectual Lucidity (G)
'One who feeds clarity from inner and outer streams'
Archangel ~ HANIEL
Capricorn / Mercury (12/22-26)

I AM THAT WHICH...

helps to bring greater clarity and understanding to dynamics with loved ones, friends and peers so that unproductive ways of relating may be healed, and relationships re-informed and re-energized. Often you hold difficult emotions about each other because certain assumptions have been made, mixed messages conveyed and misunderstandings about intent inferred. If you think ambiguity is difficult for the mind (and we notice that it often is), it can be 'torturous' for the aspiring heart – whether the aspirations are about romance, friendship, family or your place and purpose among your peers. What you feel and want with another must always be dealt with in the context of what the other feels and wants – and sometimes the other doesn't know at the moment you want them to! Hence potential frustration and confusion.

So if you want clarity about and with the other, you may need to ask questions, and be ready to hear not necessarily what you want to hear – but also perhaps something even better than you imagined! At the very least, you will likely begin to 'clear the air,' leading possibly to greater closeness because telling each other your truths creates intimacy and respect. But truth is not fixed – it changes – and it has the most potential to change when you express it. Truth allows feelings and thoughts that have been harbored inside you to be released. Sometimes when a truth of feeling or fact has been hidden for a long time, finally 'bringing it to light' enables you to realize that it isn't even your truth anymore. Or, speaking your truth affirms it and gives it wings to fly. Either way, whether truth is defined or transformed by words or action – it is set free, and so are you.

And so dear lucidity-seeking one, use my MEBAHIAH light to help you create more clarity about what you feel or want, so that you may know and convey your own truth in the moment. And then ask what the other feels or wants. In the light of dynamic conversation, or simply bringing ease to the space between you, more truth will become clearer for both of you – especially if your hearts are talking. For in these moments, remember that your hearts are not just about feeling – but insight and intuition, wisdom, compassion, forgiveness and understanding. Bring these qualities of heart to any meeting of minds – and truth and clarity will yield what is lovingly and truly true for each and all. Amen...

5/16 * 7/31 * 10/13 * **12/24** * 3/4

56 POYEL

(poi-EL)
Fortune and Support (G)
'One who taps plenitude with feeling'
Archangel ~ HANIEL
Capricorn / Moon (12/27-31)

I AM THAT WHICH...

helps you to invest in the intangible riches of family and friendship, which as these mature will multiply and yield gifts of abundance throughout lives and lifetimes. It is often when people lose material assets that they begin to count their immeasurable non-material riches. The family that loses their possessions in a fire or flood counts their blessings of survival. Many who lose limbs or certain faculties in accidents, conflict or other tragedies become grateful for what wasn't lost, as they acquire new skills and abilities and a different, but even inspiringly liveable life. Those who cannot move their entire bodies discover the richness of their minds and the miracles of compassion and care that help to sustain them. When economics are tight, even seemingly disastrous, and acquisitional powers are curbed, you begin to realize the riches you already have – both tangible and intangible – and how they may be multiplied. You learn that whatever the ebbs of life may take away, you can regenerate flow – especially working together in harmony with others to combine the riches of imagination and creativity and the eternal resources of heart and soul that you all share.

Love is creation energy – and as such there is no end to what it can restore and replenish. It is the compositional foundation of creation, and there is nothing or no one that is not composed of love. Granted, this is not so easily apparent when someone is acting in a way that expresses hurt, hate, fear or anything that divides or destroys. But know this – all beings who seem to express non-love are doing so because they _feel_ excluded from love's bounties, and are thus angry at love itself – when what they really want, even unconsciously, is to be gathered back into the inclusive and abundant embrace of care and belonging that they feel separated from.

Having the support of loved ones and peers creates such a strong sense of abundance that you become empowered to create abundance in other aspects of your life. It is like the saying, 'give a man a fish and he eats for a day, but teach him to fish and he can eat for a lifetime.' Your histories are full of those who went from nothing to something because of the faith and support of someone who believed in them. The hand of God needs the heart of humankind to do Its loving work – and you are each that heart.

Thus my supporting POYEL light dwells within you and shall proliferate as the Divine Itself among you and as you, providing all that is needed and desired. Know that each 'investment' and 'withdrawal' of light magnifies and adds to the treasure of caring and kindness amassed among you and your loved ones. And when there seems to be depletion and you don't know how to correct it – then come into the infinitude of your heart to tap the Source of all flow, that you and yours may be filled and fulfilled, again. Amen...

December 25 – 31

Angels 57 – 64

Sephira 8

HOD ~ Splendor

Overlighting Archangel

RAPHAEL ~ 'Healer-God'
(Governs with MIKHAEL) Healing,
wholeness, alchemy/transformation,
harmony, awareness.

57 NEMAMIAH

58 YEIALEL

59 HARAHEL

60 MITZRAEL

61 UMABEL

62 IAH-HEL

63 ANAUEL

64 MEHIEL

* Note that the Archangel correspondences in Sephirot 6 and 8 have been interchanged throughout the centuries by different Kabbalists and schools of thought. After additional research which shows the ways in which both Archangels are active in both Sephirot, the primary Archangel correspondences presented in the original *Birth Angels* book are reversed here, but each are included as co-governing.

5/17 * 8/1 * 10/14 * **12/25** * 3/5

57 NEMAMIAH

(neh-MA-mee-YAH)
Discernment (R)
'One who sees through the eyes of the heart'
Archangel ~ RAPHAEL (with MIKHAEL)
Capricorn / Uranus (1/1-5)

I AM THAT WHICH...

helps you to see through the eyes of your heart the gifts of infinite possibility that are present in each and all, and to grant each other the grace of time and consideration for the potential that is still unfolding. In the sameness of heart underneath all your differences, the memory of Oneness is held. Thus, when you look at others through the all-seeing light of your heart, you will see hues of your own soul's hopes and dreams in theirs, your own desire to be loved, and your own quest for a meaningful life in their search of the same. The heart sees the whole truth of a being, thus with the discernment of heart-seeing may you glimpse the eternal in the other and all that is possible which has not yet manifested. And in times of challenge know that while heart-powered discernment does not condone hurtful behavior, it allows for 'more to the story than meets the eye' and time and space for it to be revealed.

Judgment, on the other hand, is more about the judger's own self-judgment than the person being judged. If there were a 'sin' in the world, it would be judgment, for it limits and even prohibits the emergence of a person's evolving beingness in its presence – thus totally negating potential. When you exercise discernment with each other instead of judgment, you don't take each other quite so personally. You keep the possibilities open within each of you and between you by allowing facts to be fluid and truth ever evolving into new truths and more of the totality of who you are. Simply, judgment closes the door between you and another, while discernment keeps it open – because the jury of the heart is always still deliberating.

So dear heart-seeing one, allow my NEMAMIAH light to show you the love that is 'the gift which keeps on giving.' Thus may you bring love to your seeing so that the love and truth which is still in the realm of possibility may be inspired to manifest. Let love soften your observations and opinions. Consider that when beings act unloving, it is likely because they feel unloved or unbelonging – even unto themselves. Rather than a 'rush to judgment,' let there be a shift in perception. Rather than regarding only what is visible, allow what is still forming the time and generosity to take shape. Rather than being fixed in your opinions, let love eclipse them to reveal a newly birthing truth. And in your togetherness, be kind and merciful that hope may be bountiful and the 'end of a rope' always be met by an open heart and a helping hand. Think of this day as one that honors every act of love, compassion and forgiveness that one by one may heal the histories and futures of you and all who are part of you, which is all. Amen...

5/18 * 8/2 * 10/15 * **12/26** * 3/6

58 YEIALEL

(YAY-a-LEL)
Mental Force (R)
'One who lightens the heart to empower mind'
Archangel ~ RAPHAEL (with MIKHAEL)
Capricorn / Saturn (1/6-10)

I AM THAT WHICH...

helps you to harness your heart-powered intellect in relatings with others to be a force for truth, integrity and clarity of thought and purpose between and among you. Force in its positive potential is like a river of energy, a natural accumulation and strength of resources that power and empower life. Examples would be to harness the force of the wind with windmills to create energy and electricity, to harness the tides of ebb and flow caused by the moon's gravitational force on the Earth to create hydropower, or sunlight to create solar power. Every living thing and being has forces that are inherent to it – especially human beings – and each person's natural forces are unique in character, scope and focus. And so what are the forces inside you? How do you combine them into 'the force' that is ultimately your power as a Divine-Human being? How do you keep the force within you strong and accessible? And how do you harness and best use it for your own well-being and success, and in optimum relatings and collaborations with others?

The forces within you all have their origin in Divine Powers which are being continually generated into Creation.

185

Primary is the flow of Divine Love which powers your heart with feeling, insight, compassion, intuition, truth and ultimately wisdom. A second is Divine Mind, which powers your mental processes with the ability to distinguish, sort, recognize and utilize patterns and connections. A third is the life force which organizes and animates your physical matter. There are many forces in your world that propel you and your interpersonal realms and relatings, but the forces that exist inside you have the power to resist or command all the forces outside you – which includes the force of any other person acting upon or against you.

My light as YEIALEL within you is given for you to understand that your inner 'power station,' which converts Divine Energies into forces you can harness and distribute to the different parts of your being, is your heart. Not your mind – for your mind is a recipient and delegate, not a generator, of your personal force. But when you use your heart-force rightly, your mental powers can do wondrous things for yourself and others – and we stress 'for' – not 'against.' Mental force powered by the heart supports another's truth rather than intimidating or overriding it, empowers the other's power rather than overruling or stealing it, illuminates strengths rather than weaknesses, and allows space for the other to shine rather than overshadowing, bullying or tyrannizing.

Thus, dear powerfully empowered one, allow my YEIALEL light to continually clean and clear your heart so that you may tap your full measure of Divine Energies in order to be a loving, true and empowering force in the lives of others. And thus, all you are willing to give will be given unto you to do so. Amen...

5/19 + 20am * 8/3 * 10/16 * **12/27**am * 3/7

59 HARAHEL

(HA-ra-HEL)
Intellectual Richness (R)
'One who taps feeling and wisdom to enrich mind'
Archangel ~ RAPHAEL (with MIKHAEL)
Capricorn / Jupiter (1/11-15)

I AM THAT WHICH...

fosters the diversity of intellectual and creative dynamics among family, friends and peers and helps to nurture and tap the unique contributions of each rather than urging conformity. There is naturally a sense of comfort in the similarities among your 'tribes' – the one you were born into and those you form through your own partnering and childbearing, friendship and work as you progress through your life. But sameness needs the sparkle of differences that serve up the serendipitous surprises and diverse perspectives which again and again wake you up to the magic of life. As I'm sure you have noticed, most family and peer groups have one or more people who stir things up sometimes (or often!) – challenging the status quo and making everybody just uncomfortable enough to incite alternate ways of thinking and perceiving.

When you are young and still fearless, you are naturally curious about beings and ways that seem different from you. Indeed, it is in the very nature of life to seek out different forms of itself – because that is exactly what the Divine did and continues to do, as the author of life, in bringing about

Creation! And since you are made 'in the image and likeness' of the Divine, you are essentially imprinted with this same urge. You are most alive when you allow the diversity of life into the play of your consciousness and interactions with each other. This is akin to allowing all your own diverse parts – heart, mind, body and soul – to participate in creating a fully alive and dynamic life.

And so dear exemplar of life's diversity, please do use my light as HARAHEL to see the different and unusual around you as the 'spice' and opportunity in your life. By welcoming these, your thinking is diversified, awareness expanded, creativity deepened and consciousness heightened. Your whole being is enriched and you become more interesting because you are interested and engaged. Furthermore, collaborations among those who have disparate qualities and abilities often yield ideas and creations that no one of you could conjure alone. Since each of you represent a particular constellation of Divine-Human qualities, each time you cooperate with another you magnify more aspects of the Divine within human possibility, much of which still lies dormant within you. Open your mind – and your heart – to the riches of your diverse relatings, and together you will become truly and lovingly brilliant light-wands of wondrous possibility! Amen...

5/20pm + 21 * 8/4 * 10/17 * **12/27**pm * 3/8

60 MITZRAEL

(MITS-ra-EL)
Internal Reparation (R)
'One who repairs what is torn'
Archangel ~ RAPHAEL (with MIKHAEL)
Capricorn / Mars (1/16-20)

I AM THAT WHICH...

helps you to be a participant and catalyst for inner and outer healing among family, intimates and peers through conversation, patient listening and the willingness to come to a new understanding of yourself and the other. The dynamics of hurt in relationships are often rooted in long-unhealed hurts within each of the individuals involved. For example, a rejection of some kind can trigger early memories of abandonment or betrayal, and you or the other may find yourself reacting just as you did then. Whatever the seeming transgression then or now, at the heart most reactions are about the pain of feeling unloved, unseen and unappreciated. The gift of a hurtful past rearing its 'ugly head' in the present is the opportunity to call on a more experienced and wiser heart for perspective and healing. If one of you is willing to pause your own reaction, something different can happen. That 'something different' might be loving yourself enough to disengage and walk away – freed at last – or to approach the other without the projection of the past in order to have a fresh conversation in which

189

questions, rather than assumptions and associations, keep the conversation going.

Asking questions and listening to the answers can begin to unravel assumptions about what the other person means. When someone says something that triggers you, before you react defensively ask for clarification about intent or meaning. Listen for the answer. If the intent was innocent that will become clear – or if the other was speaking or acting based on the projection of their own hurts upon you, that will become clear too. Keep asking questions and listening non-reactively until old resentments are exposed – and humor and humility help to save the day! The lightening and relief to both of you will be enormous.

I offer you my MITZRAEL light to see that your relationships truly are your most fertile 'laboratories' for accelerated mutual healing. While your inner relationship with the Divine and your spiritual self cultivate the 'theories' that provide the soil for self-realization – relationships provide practical application and the interaction needed for you to blossom into fullness because of and among each other. Everything gets tested and healed in relationship. And in your relatings comes the possibility for the most profound fulfillment of all, which is to experience the fruition of individuation in the context of togetherness. You have unlimited heart-power to help each other mend your 'broken places.' Why not use it? If not you, then who? And if not now, when? Amen...

5/22 * 8/5 * 10/18 * **12/28** * 3/9

61 UMABEL

(OO-ma-BEL)
Affinity and Friendship (R)
'One who thrums the threads of interconnectedness'
Archangel ~ RAPHAEL (with MIKHAEL)
Aquarius / Sun (1/21-25)

I AM THAT WHICH...

helps you to cherish and sustain affinities with loved ones, friends and peers, even while your life paths and ways of being are expressed outwardly in many diverse ways, and to also recognize temporary or difficult affinities that offer growth and opportunity. Your relatings with others yield many different kinds of affinities, some of which last a lifetime, and some for a moment or season in your life. Those that are based on similarities and mutual appreciation, with people you feel most 'at home' with, give you a sense of belonging and comfort. Some affinities are spontaneous and exhilarating, born of synchronicity and coincidence. Other affinities are based on contrasts that help to define more clearly and uniquely who you each are and your different interests, talents and skills. Sometimes your affinities have to do with lessons that need learning and growth or healing that the deeper parts of you long for.

Your affinities and friendships are the pull of your souls to each other in order that your beingness may be defined and revealed, expressed and expanded, honed and healed. Oneness without differentiation and diversity is a theoretical

191

life, for not in the Heavens nor the Earth nor in all the universes can any being be known fully to itself without a reflective and co-creative other. Just as your human existence reflects and expresses the inherent diversity of the Divine Being, you and each person in your life play sacred roles of reflection for each other. Your affinities provide a spiritual map for your life journey – even when the affinity expresses as an antipathy – for both affinities and antipathies are clues to your true identity and soul purposes.

I invite you to feel the affinity of my UMABEL light for your own light as the affinity of the Divine for the Human which renders you as a uniquely-configured Divine-Human being. Thus respect your affinities with loved ones in the roles you play in each other's lives as mother, father, sister, brother, daughter, son, niece, nephew and so on – but also be curious about them, ask questions about what they feel or think without assuming you know the answer. In being present with each other without assumptions or hidden agendas, your affinities may be deepened and the potential for creating something new together heightened. Let my light help you to remember again and again that however different each of you may be, your essential affinity may be found in your sameness of heart – in your desire to love and be loved and to have a meaningful and worthwhile life. And know that whenever you are joined with another through an affinity of heart, all the Angels, all that is Divine, rejoice with infinite gladness. Amen...

5/23 * 8/6 * 10/19 * **12/29** * 3/10

62 IAH-HEL

(EE-a-HEL)
Desire to Know (R)
'One who calls you to the unknown'
Archangel ~ RAPHAEL (with MIKHAEL)
Aquarius / Venus (1/26-30)

I AM THAT WHICH...

helps to cultivate a desire and willingness to know others, to collaborate with others toward that which you desire to know, to share truly and wisely what you already know – and to know that for all you know, there is so very much more still to know which may be known only by your heart and between one heart and another. One of your greatest and most constant urges as a Divine-Human being is to know – and it is driven both by an infinite curiosity about life and also the desire to feel more at home on your Earth, in your immediate surroundings and especially with each other. It is this desire to know which ensures your ongoing vibrancy and vitality, not only within yourself, but with all others. In addition to mutual love and kindness, the desire to know each other is what continually revitalizes those who are lifelong partners and friends – for each know that the other is always growing and unfolding. Thus, thinking that you know all there is to know about each other – and ceasing to explore your respective and mutual depths and dreamings, thoughts and feelings – essentially deadens life and creativity between you. And what's the fun of that!

All that is juicy about life, love and mutuality is found in the depths – in the quality of knowing, rather than the quantity. True knowing is not about how much you know, but how well. Some people have a thousand casual friends, and they remain strangers not only to each other, but to themselves in each other's presence. On the other hand, have you ever experienced an encounter with a stranger who came to know you better in your brief sojourn together than many of your long-time intimates? If you are partnered, do you still ask each other probing questions and listen for the answers the way you did when you first met? You do if you understand that both of you are still and always growing – even moreso for your continuing interest in each other. For to be with someone who truly desires to know you brings that much more of who you are into the light to become knowable.

I, IAH-HEL, tell you that when you dare to know each other, you dare to co-create your lives together. You dare to enter into the greater knowing of the heart and the remembering of the soul. You dare to know that first moment in timelessness when the Divine Oneness became Two and each saw Itself in the Other. In daring to truly and deeply know each other, you dare to know why Creation came about, and which part of the Divine "I Am" you each are. In daring to know each other through the all-knowing of love, any truth about each of you is knowable as an expression of love. Amen...

5/24 * 8/7 * 10/20 * **12/30** * 3/11

63 ANAUEL

(a-NA-oo-EL)
Perception of Unity (S)
'One who sees the Oneness within the many'
Archangel ~ RAPHAEL (with MIKHAEL)
Aquarius / Mercury (1/31-2/4)

I AM THAT WHICH...

helps you to realize in your relatings and relationships the samenesses of heart which reflect the unity underlying your differences and diversities. Your physical appearance, style, manner of speaking, thought processes and more are unique to you. There is no one else who looks and acts like you, no one who thinks or speaks about the same things in the same ways you do. However, in your heart of hearts, all human beings pretty much want the same thing – to love and be loved and to be truly yourself in a meaningful, purposeful way that connects you to each other and the whole. Although who, how and what you choose to fulfill these desires differ, the goals are the same. No matter where or how you live – in cityscapes, farms, tribal deserts, tropical jungles, remote islands or distant mountains – partnering, family-making and peer-grouping are universal to your humanity, as is purposing your lives through creativity, education, expertise and enterprise. Ideally, personal becoming enlivens and enriches the whole, such as family and community – so that the whole can become stronger and better able to support its members, providing a sense of worthwhileness and belonging to each and all.

However far afield you may venture from your family and 'tribal groups' in your personal individuation, you are periodically drawn home again, to those who represent your origin and sense of belonging. You experience this especially during holidays, holy days and important rites of passage, when you partake of the magnified light of gathering, commemoration and celebration within the diversity and oneness of family, friendships and circles that ripple beyond. For it is the circle of unity which you came from and the circles of unity which you create that give your individuation meaning. It is this same urge toward home and togetherness that drives the soul within you to seek its own 'heavenly' origin and to create a time and place of belonging on Earth that re-enacts a sense of the eternal and the unity of oneness.

Thus, dear diverse one within the oneness of all, I invite you to partake of my ANAUEL light to never lose sight of the oneness from which your uniqueness is born. For all your diverse worldly adventures, it is your inner realm – the world of heart and soul – that holds the memory and sacred space of oneness within you. And thus in your circles of loved ones and peers may you be reminded of this as you return to your sameness of heart to practice unity even in your seeming separateness of body and being. May your shared inner realms inform and give meaning to your outer creations so that your aspirations be noble and generous, always remembering that whatever hurt or healing is done to one is done to all. And may you let the love of the Divine for you be as your love for each other and life itself. Amen...

5/25 * 8/8 * 10/21 * **12/31** * 3/12

64 MEHIEL

(MAY-hee-EL)
Vivification (Invigorate & Enliven) (G)
'One who brings the elixir of life to the vessel'
Archangel ~ RAPHAEL (with MIKHAEL)
Aquarius / Moon (2/5-9)

I AM THAT WHICH...

helps to enliven and re-enliven relationships with a spirit of mutual discovery, appreciation, enthusiasm, and the willingness to allow each other to change and grow – and also be different from you. Possibly the most enlivening aspect of life is change. Change is what keeps your life moving and interesting by bringing on the new and different. Change triggers your potential to reveal and evolve more of the truth of yourself and become more fine-tuned in your being and doing. And with change you get to practice being more and more of who you are in different scenarios with always evolving others.

As much as you may seek out those with whom you share common affinities, you are often more enriched and broadened by those who differ from you. (Yet some points of commonality do allow you to feel more comfortable with the differences of the other.) There is often at least one person in a family or peer group who is 'more different' than the rest. And whether that person is the scapegoat, the 'black sheep,' the underachiever, genius, rebel or 'star performer,' this is the person in the group who can keep things just exciting or uncomfortable enough to catalyze the most growth and expansion for all. The key is for your interest and curiosity to be greater than your need for things and beings to be the same – as in what you already know and understand. In the willingness to step beyond your 'comfort zone' to query and explore, you and all involved can be enlivened to new levels of individual and communal aliveness and vitality.

Diverse circles of family, friends and colleagues can be fertile gardens for planting new seeds of discovery and cultivating adventurous terrains of co-creativity, knowledge and achievement. Ideally, every person on a team is valued for their different talent or skill that is complementary to the whole – which is readily apparent in sports, science, music, education and organizations of all kinds. Think of your family, friends and peers in the same way, as a team or group of teams, with each member contributing something unique and valuable that enlivens and enriches the whole. And all the while, notice with whom you feel most alive, most or even more yourself, most interested in life – and stoke those fires!

So dear alive one who thrives on the different (for truly you do!), use my MEHIEL light to see how precious and important are your differences, how you are vitalized and renewed by each other's growth and evolution. Rather than being intimidated by strength, uniqueness or 'star-quality' – and shrinking back or trying to trim the other's edges, clip wings or curb ways – be inspirations and helpers to each other. Be curious, admiring and appreciative, and see how much more of your own self is inspired to emerge! For the more yourself you are, the more truly alive you can be with, for, to and among others. Amen...

January 1 – 8

Angels 65 – 72

Sephira 9
YESOD ~ Foundation

Overlighting Archangel
GABRIEL ~ 'God is my Strength'
Guidance, vision, inspiration for faith
and connection to the Divine; vessel for
giving and receiving, creative fertility,
and the ebb and flow of life's seasons

---

65 DAMABIAH
66 MANAKEL
67 EYAEL
68 HABUHIAH
69 ROCHEL
70 JABAMIAH
71 HAIYAEL
72 MUMIAH

65 DAMABIAH

(da-MA-bee-YAH)
Fountain of Wisdom (R)
'One who brings the ocean to the river'
Archangel ~ GABRIEL
Aquarius / Uranus (2/10-14)

I AM THAT WHICH...

helps you to become wise in your relatings by seeing each other in the love-light of a more whole truth. Anything you may think you know about another, any 'truth' you may observe or 'believe' or 'swear by,' is only part-truth unless you are looking through the eyes of your heart. For your heart sees not only what is here, but also what is on its way, even a hope or dream of being or doing that is still forming and not yet visible – like the seed in winter's ground. The wisdom of love not only sees all, but in that seeing has the power to inspire more of that 'all' from the eternal where the totality of a soul originates, into time where it may be manifested. Just as the light of the sun will coax the seedling out of the cold dark earth into the warmth of Spring.

In the context of your relatings, it is this heart-seeing of potential that often draws you to another. When it is sometimes said about two people in a relationship, 'I don't know what she sees in him' – it may be that she has fallen in love with his potential! If she loves him, she sees his totality, but the greater wisdom of her heart must help her to see that only part of who he is has manifested in time – and it may take a lot more time for the rest of him to show up in this reality! For truly love may inspire the manifestation of potential in another, but it will not force it. As a human being, your earthly reality of time and place is important to you on so many levels. But you are not only human – you are a Divine-Human being, as are all. Thus, the wisdom in measuring the viability of your earthly reality is to know if it is conducive also to your soul reality – and if you are living your life among those who inspire or inhibit your soul expression and purpose.

The wisdom of the heart exercised among you shows love commingled with intuition, insight, compassion, understanding, and when needed, the grace of forgiveness. Heart-wisdom is also about acceptance and respect for another's truth and timing along their journey of individuation. If what you want from others is what they want for themselves, your relating will have integrity, depth and possibility. Practicing wisdom enables you to dissolve oppositional dynamics by understanding that in working together in love and truth, all may receive what it is that each truly wants – which is the freedom to love and create a meaningful life in a way that most speaks to and from your hearts. And in the deeper mysteries of truth-in-relationship, what is true for one helps to inspire or release what is true for the other in one way or another – even if it hurts at first.

For all this my wisdom-light as DAMABIAH is given to dwell within you so that every approach may be the seed of a new beginning. Whenever you desire to better understand another and to begin anew, look through the eyes of love. Listen and receive, seek and you shall find the other's heart – and a more whole truth will emerge for both of you. Amen...

5/27 * 8/10 * 10/23 * **1/2** * 3/14

66 MANAKEL

(MA-na -KEL)
Knowledge of Good and Evil (R)
'One who lights a candle to cure the darkness'
Archangel ~ GABRIEL
Aquarius / Saturn (2/15-19)

I AM THAT WHICH...

helps you to broaden your perceptions of 'good' or 'bad, and to see how the contrast of these in your relatings with each other moves your life forward through change, learning, growth, and opportunities for greater awareness and healing. The concepts of good and bad – and even the 'baddest bad' which you call 'evil' – are formed by the values held by you and your loved ones, peers and social groups, as well as your own innate sense of right and wrong, hurting or helping, good and bad, acceptable and not acceptable – which are all influenced by the moralities espoused in your cultural/communal value systems and religions.

In the context of interpersonal relatings, your beliefs and perceptions about good and bad affect the way you treat each other and how you define and react to good or bad acts. You naturally see as good those acts which affirm what you want to experience in your life, and bad acts as things you do not want to experience. However, as likely anyone knows who has survived the 'misfortune' of disappointment, illness, tragedy, loss and more, new possibilities begin to show up once grief and resistance to what happened begin to give way to surrender and even some acceptance. It is the nature of love and life to fill a void, and whatever you may suffer you have that 'on your side.' Even if everything is different than before, new ways bring new life – and often new love and purpose – which can happen after losing a job or going through a separation or death of a loved one.

Value judgments also play into what you assume and want from or for each other. What is perceived to be good or bad for one is not always good or bad for another. One may feel it is good to have a home and family and a steady job, while another may feel it is good to be free to travel the world, doing different jobs with diverse friendships and relatings. Parents may feel it is good for their child to go to college and maybe even pursue a specific course of study, while the child (who is striving toward adulthood and emancipation) may want to play in a rock band. Neither choice is good or bad – and both choices are opportunities to grow and learn and discover more of who one truly is – which means that any choice is ultimately a good choice if it leads to the realization of one's own love and truth of being.

With choices that bring harm to oneself or another, recognizing these as symptoms of the need for healing is the first step in creating good from a 'bad' event. There is nothing that happens on Earth that does not have the potential for the expansion of love, light, truth and greater awareness for all. Dysfunction, disease, and other destructive conditions can fester and undermine positive potential at deep and hidden levels – but they ultimately erupt on the surface to show that healing is needed – and possible. One person's bad or harmful act is a potential that exists not only within the dynamics of their community – but all humankind, which sometimes wakes up a family or community to changes and healing needed for issues too long ignored. Your healers and therapeutic helpers know this, which is why they invite a whole family to participate in the healing of the one who is in obvious need. Or they offer their services to an entire community when there has been a public tragedy that has affected everyone in different ways.

Many of you disavow the existence of a 'higher power' that would allow children and other innocents to be harmed. But by negating anything you don't understand or can't see, you cut yourselves off from the very realms in which your 'invisible helpers' dwell – and especially the resources in your own inner realms of heart and soul which enable you to overcome and transform negative events. Your soul carries a holographic 'tincture' of your Oneness-origin and the Divine Itself as your soul-parent – which is conveyed to your heart through love, compassion, 'inner-tuitions' and wisdom. But in giving the gift of free will to the life that comes out of Itself – just as you do with your own children – God has empowered you as Its 'offspring' to make your own choices and follow your own paths of communion and creation.

Thus, in the paradoxical gift of free will, both aspects of light are yours to choose – the flow and presence of light, or its seeming ebb or absence. Both are necessary to the comings and goings of life, for example, when a season of change calls you into the darker humus of your being in order to gestate and nurture seeds of potential. But just as the Divine knows the whole 'circle-truth' about the souls it engenders, there is nothing in all the universes that does not ultimately return to the light. Choosing the dark is sometimes just the long way around to get there!

A full and 'good' life is a mixture of inner and outer life. You draw from the inner, which is the life-sustaining eternal light within your heart and soul that is God-the-Oneness with omnipotent potential – to go toward your outer life, which is God-diversified into physicality, choice and the potency of creativity within seeming limitation. 'Evil' is going so far into the outer life that there is a forgetting and even negating of the life-affirming values held by the inner, and thus creation energies are inverted and used to destroy and harm. The power in your Divine-Human beingness is that if you are willing to continually return to the Divine Oneness held within your heart and soul, you will know how to go back out into life while taking the light of God with you.

Thus do I, MANAKEL, suggest to not separate yourselves from each other in judgments of good and evil, but recognize that the opportunities and challenges of one are those of all of you, in one way or another. Whatever your transgressions might ever be against others or others against you, your 'salvation' is always to return to the love, truth and compassion which proceed from the Divine dwelling within you. Thus, you may infuse light and love into even the darkest situations, and the darkness will pass, having no lasting hold on you. For life's deepest urges are to move toward the light. While the seemingly darker times of contraction or emptying out may feel bad, unfortunate, unlucky or even tragic, if you can 'look at the dark in a different light, you will always see the dawn lying in wait.' So dear one, do not do battle against the dark, but rather just 'let there be light,' again and again. Amen...

5/28 * 8/11 * 10/24 * **1/3** * 3/15

67 EYAEL

(AY-ya -EL)
Transformation to the Sublime (R)
'One who illumines the inner star'
Archangel ~ GABRIEL
Pisces / Jupiter (2/20-24)

I AM THAT WHICH...

helps you to take your relationships 'up a notch' by seeing the Divine in the human and the miracle in the mundane – and by using changing and challenging energies between you as a prompt to expand the light. Your heart is a communication and energy bridge between the lighter resonances of your soul and the denser vibrations of your body. This is because your heart is the meeting place between the Divine and the Human, the 'Above' and 'Below,' the sublime and material reality. The Divine Light in every human heart longs to ground the higher spheres of love and truth into the humus of your humanity. Thus, whenever you desire to heighten your relatings with another, let your heart meet the heart of the other and allow the light and love within each to be quickened and commingled. Thus may you be transported together to a 'higher' way of being in each other's presence. While lofty intellectual concepts or philosophies can inspire the individual, it is the love and light exchanged between hearts that has the most profound impact on not just 'knowing better,' but being and doing better individually and together.

The greatest gift you can give to others is to see the light that they are, for in the seeing, their light quickens and expands so that they can more truly and lovingly see and be themselves. On the other hand, if someone does not seem to see you – rather than identifying with their 'blind spot' – visit your own higher inner vista and see yourself as the Angels within see you. And when you are accosted by someone's darker energies, rather than defending yourself or descending into self-judgment or attack of the other – seek out any shadows within you that might be attracting their darkness, and draw on the light within your heart to displace the dark.

And thus, my transporting light as EYAEL is always within to illuminate for you how to heighten your own presence and the dynamics within your relationships by tapping your soul's resources held within your heart. Bring anything you think you know about the other into the ruminations of your heart, where love and wisdom prevail, and you will discover a more whole truth about the other and yourself. If you are teaching another, awaken the light-teacher within their own heart, and let you both be willing to learn. When parenting your children, love and support them, and they will more quickly and deeply learn what is true and right for them – and thereby come to you to see themselves more clearly. When partnering with and befriending each other, see and encourage the unique expressions of light within and between you and cherish your differences as different 'angles' of the same light. And finally, see your difficult human behaviors as the "antics of Angels with folded wings" – and love each other anyway so that wings may unfurl in sky-high togetherness! Amen...

5/29 * 8/12 * 10/25 * **1/4** * 3/16

68 HABUHIAH

(ha-BU-hee-YAH)
Healing (R)
'One who loves hurt into healing'
Archangel ~ GABRIEL
Pisces / Mars (2/25-29)

I AM THAT WHICH...

helps you to use any difficulties, harbored hurts or resentments with loved ones, friends and peers as gifts of illumination to show where healing is needed within yourself, and to let your own healing be the beginning of healing with others. It is very natural to blame another for hurting you and to see them as the cause of your hurt. However, often a hurtful act to you is actually just 'poking' at a hurt that already resides within you, as you say, like 'pouring salt on a wound.' For example, the degree of pain, even devastation, you may feel if your partner leaves you may be re-activating a hurt early in your life when one of your parents left. When the new hurt is deep, you may also be too consumed with compounded grief to realize that your partner's leaving might be less about you and more about an old hurt of their own that got triggered in your relationship – and perhaps the leaving was a gift for reasons not yet apparent. Betrayal is also common in partnerships, and when it happens it could be fulfilling a long-held fear of betrayal – or the betrayal of some truth within oneself. In each case, the underlying gift is the opportunity for awareness and self-healing. The other's action is on them. Your reaction is on you – and you have the unlimited resources of heart and soul to heal anything.

So much of what you react to as an adult is origined in your childhood. When you are children, you do not know the histories and travails of your parents. That is as it should be, because the gift of your birth is meant to lighten and increase love and joy in their lives, and the joy of youth is to be unencumbered by the past. However, sometimes the weight and pain of your parents' own past is too heavy and their wounds may be re-visited upon you, which you then may carry into your own adulthood. Resentment can grow in both generations, which left unhealed can be passed down for many more. We offer this bit of light for understanding: most hurts are about feeling unloved. If you look at others beyond the roles you have expected them to fulfill in your life, you will realize that more than explanations, excuses or analysis, what is needed most is love.

Thus, dear one, I shine my light within you as HAHUHIAH to help you begin the healing for those before and around you by healing yourself. Since long-harbored hurts tend to fester in the heart, your heart is where healing must and can most potently happen. The resources of your heart are unlimited. As the receiver of your soul-light, your heart can access the eternal to mend all emotional bruises and brokenness in time. Therefore, approach all hurt with heart, in giving and receiving. And let the healing begin. Amen...

5/30 * 8/13 * 10/26 * **1/5** * 3/17

69 ROCHEL

(ro-SHEL)

Restitution (R)

'One who brings back your lost parts'

Archangel ~ GABRIEL

Pisces / Sun (3/1-5)

I AM THAT WHICH...

helps you to understand the karmic opportunities with people and relationships lost or recovered, and how to offer and receive restitution by restoring truth, wholeness and unity within and between you. The natural ebb and flow of life is such that people and relationships will be lost to you at times. Sometimes they may be re-found through new perspectives and personal transformations, or others will come to fill what has been emptied in a new way. Often where there has been loss, there is a strong desire or need for things to 'be like they were before,' to restore what you 'once had' or to 'get back to normal.' But the true treasures of living are not found in things staying the same – as comforting as that may seem. Indeed, trying to make things stay the same is often what causes disruption and loss in relationships. Relationships need to have fluidity and flexibility because individuals need to keep individuating toward personal truth and purpose, which in turn naturally evolves and enriches the dynamics of relationship. Thus it's a good idea to keep your relationships in 'stretch pants!'

Sometimes when a loved one is lost, there can be a feeling that they have taken part of you with them, which renders you partially lost as well. This is natural because you play different roles and share unique aspects of yourself with each person in your life. If your only child is lost, then suddenly your role as mother or father is also lost. If your spouse is lost, then suddenly you are no longer a wife or husband. If a 'best friend' is lost, suddenly you are no longer a best friend yourself. The human psyche can hardly bear loss, and something must be restored in order to heal and go on with life. Thus, much of the true and deeper healing needed in lost and broken relationships is not to bring that person back, but to bring you back to yourself. When your own truth of being is restored, you will be able to come back into life and new relatings with a deepened, more loving, wise and whole beingness.

Thus my restorative light as ROCHEL is given so that you may always return to yourself, and thereby return a more whole and true self to your relatings, again and again. Nothing or no one can take what truly belongs to you, and so, ultimately what is restored is not that which was taken, but that which you gave away. The only thing you can give away and yet never lose is love. So when you give yourself 'away' in relationship let it be an act of love, in fulfillment of love, from the truth of who you are – not as self-sacrifice or self-diminishment, or as a contract for a specific exchange. For it is in the ever-present presence of love and truth that all restitution is made, not only in the present, but to the past and the future – whether a particular relationship survives or not in time. Finally, in the Allness of the eternal beyond time, no one is ever lost if you allow what they brought to your life to live on in the foreverness of your heart. Amen...

5/31 * 8/14 * 10/27 * **1/6** * 3/18

70 JABAMIAH

(ya-BA-mee-YAH)
Alchemy (Transformation) (R)
'One who turns base mettle into gold'
Archangel ~ GABRIEL
Pisces / Venus (3/6-10)

_____

I AM THAT WHICH...

helps you to be a transformative presence in your relationships through love, acceptance, truth, empathy, compassion – and your own willingness to be transformed. Your relatings with each other help you to define, form and transform yourselves – not by seeking the other's change, but your own. While you may not condone another's behavior or choices – your acceptance rather than judgment of who they are in that moment can be the first step in the transformation of each of you and the relationship itself. Not having to react to your resistance or judgment provides a space for the other's self-assessment to emerge naturally. In the meantime, 'being the change you want to see,' as you say, can have a profound effect on your interpersonal dynamics, since focusing on your own transformation often has a 'side effect' of energetically inspiring awareness and change in the other – even if they are a world away.

For example, if you want the other person to be more caring and thoughtful of you, first become moreso with yourself. By loving and embracing yourself, you will not only set a 'standard' of desirable treatment, but you will also

213

begin to feel more empathy with the other's concerns and circumstances. Thus there will be no resentment, and it will be easier to approach with what you desire and also what you can give. This vibratory change in you will energetically invoke a compatible response in the other, sooner or later – or – the person may go away, 'killed by kindness,' because they cannot meet your more loving vibration at that time! Either way, truths and transformations will occur between you, and you will both be changed for the better, each in your own way and time according to the needs of your whole being.

My transformative light as JABAMIAH is given unto you so that you might bring the love-and-truth 'gold' of your own inner being into your relatings with others – both friend and seeming 'foe' – thereby doing your part to ennoble what is possible between and among you. Ultimately, where there is love, honesty and integrity, an alchemical reaction of change occurs within and between you which is greater than the sum of you – for here shall the Divine rise up from within and between each of you to meet and compound Itself in the other. This is how true 'church' or 'temple' happens among you, at the altar of your hearts in soul-communion. Amen...

6/1 * 8/15 * 10/28 * **1/7** * 3/19

71 HAIYAEL

(HA-ee-ya-EL)
Divine Warrior & Weaponry (R)
'One who wins the battle that cannot be fought'
Archangel ~ GABRIEL
Pisces / Mercury (3/11-15)

I AM THAT WHICH...

helps you to be a stand for love, integrity and truth in your relatings with others without having to do battle. There is no battle that can win you the war, no matter what you are fighting for. Anything worth winning can only be given, not taken. And the only thing truly worth having, after all, is the one thing you can never lose – and that is love. For the more you give it away, the more you have. The challenge in your life as a human is to remember this. On Earth, you think more in terms of having or not having the things you desire, especially love. But the truth is that love is always here – it never leaves, but only changes form. It is up to you to recognize it, which you can only do by looking with your heart. When you do battle with each other, you are not in your heart and thus not able see it.

The human part of your Divine-Human beingness forgets that you are each and all aspects of manifested love. You cannot win or fight for each other's love, because you cannot make someone else see or feel or want you. All you can do is to increase the visible presence of the love that you are – and allow others to see or not see you according to

215

their own capacity at that time and what part of them is doing the looking.

Dear emotional gladiators, if you must take each other on – use my HAIYAEL warrior-light not to fight the other, but to illuminate the hurting places that cause either of you to strike out at the other. And in the fiery commingling of Divine-Human light, let the swords and shields between you, which keep you from seeing and being seen, be melted down! And also with my HAIYAEL light, see yourself and each other as we do from all the 'angles' of Divine Love and Light that we are. In everything you do we see possibility and purpose. In your every hurting place we see your potential for healing. In your every dark moment we see you simply not seeing the light within. See your own hue in our all-encompassing light, and howevermuch another may be looking at you 'through a glass darkly,' your light will keep steady until it seeks and finds itself in the heart of the other. Then, truly, as you say, you can "make love, not war." Amen...

6/2 * 8/16 * 10/29 * **1/8** * 3/20

72 MUMIAH

(MOO-mee-YAH)
Endings and Rebirth (R)
'One who uses endings to begin again'
Archangel ~ GABRIEL
Pisces / Moon (3/16-20)

I AM THAT WHICH...

helps you to 'let go' of each other again and again, so that new creation energies may proliferate within and among you and bring rebirth to your individualities and relationships. As much as you may want each other and your relationships to stay the same, you must grow and change in order to continually move toward your personal truths, life paths and purposes – and keep your relationships vibrant. Life's most basic urge is to evolve from what-was to the new that desires to come into being. Extracting the 'juice' of yesterday in every new today will allow you to harvest a newborn tomorrow that is rich and fertile with infinite possibilities.

Between endings and new beginnings there is often a period of what you call 'regrouping' – a time of seeming dormancy when energies and aspects are regathering and reassembling, and when it may seem like nothing is happening because it is not yet visible. You feel this with a shift in a relationship from what was to something new that is still forming. Sometimes you even need to grow certain aspects of yourself away from those who are particularly

217

influential in your life. As with a newborn seedling, some ligh is too bright or winds too strong for new parts of yourself that may be trying to emerge – which is why gardeners use small 'starter' pots for certain vulnerable seeds. To allow your relationships to change, gestate or 'take a break' without feeling anxious or resentful is to respect the passages of life within, between and among you. No one cultivates truth of self to spite another – but encouraging each other's truths may ultimately bring you closer.

As you say in different ways – if you have love enough to let go, what truly belongs to you will return in one way or another. Nowhere do you see this more profoundly than with your children in the cultivation of their individualities, or in long-time friendships that ebb and flow. Sometimes the return does not come in the same way or from the person that precipitated the loss – as with the case of 'broken' relationships with partners. But the letting go, which respects the self-sovereignty of others and yourself, is vital to being able to bring the gifts of yesterday into tomorrow.

So dear one, use my light as MUMIAH to allow the endings that are 'game-changers' in your relatings with others. Whether endings between you are about transforming old unproductive dynamics into new ways of relating, or accepting temporary or permanent loss of them – if you allow their essence to always be in your heart you will never truly lose what was important between you. All losses prepare the way for new life. Howevermuch sorrow there may be for awhile, you are 'hardwired' for new beginnings. For all comings and goings are meant for the ongoingness of life and the opportunity for new expressions of love and truth within and among you. Amen...

Sephira 10

MALKUTH (SHEKINAH)

Relates to the Kingdom of Creation

and the Realm of Saints and Ascended Souls

Overlighting Archangels

SANDALPHON and METATRON

These two Archangels, sometimes referred to as "spiritual brothers," are arguably said to be the only two Archangels who were once human and taken up to the heavens without having experienced human death: METATRON was Enoch, and SANDALPHON was Elijah. Metatron's unmanifested creation energies in KETHER are finally manifest in MALKUTH and the SHEKINAH (feminine aspect of the Divine) which gives birth to Earth. Thus here METATRON is the link between the Divine and all of humanity, while SANDALPHON is the overlighting Archangel of the Earth, planetary "caretaker" who grounds Divine Love within humanity and the natural world in order to cultivate higher consciousness on Earth.

In the Tree of Life symbology Sephira 10 is a "bridge" realm leading from the Angelic Heavens to Earth, the realm of saints and ascended souls. Therefore, there are no Angels (except Archangels) correspondent to this last Sephira of the Tree. However, it is included here in order to complete the spiritual descent of the Heavenly Tree of Life unto Earth as it takes root and branches out into, within and among the hearts of all humanity.

Amen...Amen...Amen

Appendix I
Your Personal Birth Angels

The ancient mysteries reveal that our souls come to Earth for many lifetimes in order to heal the unhealed hurts and issues that occur in human life, which we call our "karma," so that we might advance the "dharma" of our soul purposes in service to the expansion of the Divine within ourselves and others. Because of the density and forgetfulness of Earth-life, it is said that in our choosing of circumstances for each lifetime we also choose certain influences, guides and cosmic aspects around our time of birth that will act as symbols or "signatures" to remind us what we came here to do. Similarly, the 72 Angels reveal that through their hierarchies of relationship to Creation and time, we also are "assigned" – or choose – a constellation of particular Angelic Energies to dwell with and within us whose qualities of Divine love-and-light-consciousness correspond to our soul purposes and challenges for this lifetime. While a kind of hologram of all 72 Angels are imprinted within us, we are especially attended by the three Angels that were the supporting energies at the moment we were born, who throughout our lives help to quicken and amplify the spark of Divinity carried within our soul and its expression in time, meaning and matter. Our Birth Angels take on these roles as they work with the physical, emotional and mental aspects of our being:

Your **Incarnation Angel** ~ Expresses qualities of the Divine Being and Will through human physical existence, will and life purpose. Corresponds to your five-day period of birth and supports the qualities, challenges and expressions of your physical being and your soul purposes throughout your human lifetime.

Your **Heart Angel** ~ Expresses qualities of Divine Love through the feelings and wisdoms of the human heart. Corresponds to your actual day of birth, your emotional qualities, challenges and potentials, and supports the cultivation of personal truth and wisdom, as well as love, compassion, forgiveness and understanding for self and others.

Your **Intellect Angel** ~ Expresses qualities of Divine Mind through the constructs and creations of human intelligence. Corresponds to your time of birth (within 20 minutes), your mental qualities, challenges and potentials and the cultivation of greater awareness and higher-mind. <u>Those born at a cusp time (on the hour or 20 minutes before or after) have two Intellect Angels (for a total of four Birth Angels)</u>. (See p. 225 for your Intellect Angel(s).)

You can know who your Birth Angels are by corresponding your day and time of birth to the Angels' days and times of influence. (See below, as well as *The 72 Angels of the Tree of Life* quick-reference chart at www.terahcox.com/birth-angels.html). I would like to clarify the use of the terms "govern," "influence" and "support." The Angels are spoken of as governing certain days and times, as well as the different planes of human beingness (physical, emotional and mental). What is meant by the term governing here is *influence, correspondence* and *support*. Ideally, because of our Divinely-endowed birthright of free will, we humans govern ourselves and support each other (an arguable concept!). The Angels, therefore, are not within and among us to govern us, but to bring a positive influence of Divine energies and support for our highest good – which is to amplify and magnify the truth of who we each uniquely are and support the fruition of our soul purposes and potentials in time and eternity.

The 72 Angels' Days of Incarnation Support

Your Incarnation Angel expresses the Divine Being and Will in human physical existence, will and life purpose. Their dates of governing correspond to the five-day period around your birth and the qualities, challenges and expressions of your physical being and purpose.

3/21 - 25	1 VEHUIAH – Will & New Beginnings
3/26 - 30	2 JELIEL – Love & Wisdom
3/31 – 4/4	3 SITAEL – Construction of Worlds
4/5 – 9	4 ELEMIAH – Divine Power
4/10 – 14	5 MAHASIAH – Rectification
4/15 – 20	6 LELAHEL – Light of Understanding

4/21 – 25	7	ACHAIAH – Patience
4/26 – 30	8	CAHETEL – Divine Blessings
5/1 – 5	9	HAZIEL – Divine Mercy & Forgiveness
5/6 – 10	10	ALADIAH – Divine Grace
5/11 – 15	11	LAUVIAH – Victory
5/16 – 20	12	HAHAIAH – Refuge/Shelter
5/21 – 25	13	YEZALEL – Fidelity, Loyalty, Allegiance
5/26 – 31	14	MEBAHEL – Truth, Liberty, Justice
6/1 – 5	15	HARIEL – Purification
6/6 – 10	16	HAKAMIAH – Loyalty
6/11 – 15	17	LAVIAH – Revelation
6/16 – 21	18	CALIEL – Justice
6/22 – 26	19	LEUVIAH – Expansive Intelligence, Fruition
6/27 – 7/1	20	PAHALIAH – Redemption
7/2 – 6	21	NELCHAEL – Ardent Desire to Learn
7/7 – 11	22	YEIAYEL – Fame/Renown
7/12 – 16	23	MELAHEL – Healing Capacity
7/17 – 22	24	HAHEUIAH – Protection
7/23 – 27	25	NITH-HAIAH – Spiritual Wisdom & Magic
7/28 – 8/1	26	HAAIAH – Political Science & Ambition
8/2 – 6	27	YERATEL – Propagation of the Light
8/7 – 12	28	SEHEIAH – Longevity
8/13 – 17	29	REIYEL – Liberation
8/18 – 22	30	OMAEL – Fertility, Multiplicity
8/23 – 28	31	LECABEL – Intellectual Talent
8/29 – 9/2	32	VASARIAH – Clemency & Equilibrium
9/3 – 7	33	YEHUIAH – Subordination to Higher Order
9/8 – 12	34	LEHAHIAH – Obedience
9/13 – 17	35	CHAVAKIAH – Reconciliation
9/18 – 23	36	MENADEL – Inner/Outer Work
9/24 – 28	37	ANIEL – Breaking the Circle
9/29 – 10/3	38	HAAMIAH – Ritual & Ceremony
10/4 – 8	39	REHAEL – Filial Submission
10/9 – 13	40	YEIAZEL – Divine Consolation & Comfort
10/14 – 18	41	HAHAHEL – Mission
10/19 – 23	42	MIKAEL – Political Authority & Order
10/24 – 28	43	VEULIAH – Prosperity
10/29 – 11/2	44	YELAHIAH – Karmic Warrior

11/3 – 7	45 SEALIAH – Motivation & Willfulness
11/8 – 12	46 ARIEL – Perceiver & Revealer
11/13 – 17	47 ASALIAH – Contemplation
11/18 – 22	48 MIHAEL – Fertility & Fruitfulness
11/23 – 27	49 VEHUEL – Elevation & Grandeur
11/28 – 12/2	50 DANIEL – Eloquence
12/3 – 7	51 HAHASIAH – Universal Medicine
12/8 – 12	52 IMAMIAH – Expiation of Errors
12/13 – 16	53 NANAEL – Spiritual Communication
12/17 – 21	54 NITHAEL – Rejuvenation & Eternal Youth
12/22 – 26	55 MEBAHIAH – Intellectual Lucidity
12/27 – 1/31	56 POYEL – Fortune & Support
1/1 – 5	57 NEMAMIAH – Discernment
1/6 – 10	58 YEIALEL – Mental Force
1/11 – 15	59 HARAHEL – Intellectual Richness
1/16 – 20	60 MITZRAEL – Internal Reparation
1/21 – 25	61 UMABEL – Affinity & Friendship
1/26 – 30	62 IAH– HEL – Desire to Know
1/31 – 2/4	63 ANAUEL – Perception of Unity
2/5 – 9	64 MEHIEL – Vivification (Invigorate/Enliven)
2/10 – 14	65 DAMABIAH – Fountain of Wisdom
2/15 – 19	66 MANAKEL – Knowledge of Good & Evil
2/20 – 24	67 EYAEL – Transformation to Sublime
2/25 – 29	68 HABUHIAH – Healing
3/1 – 5	69 ROCHEL – Restitution
3/6 – 10	70 JABAMIAH – Alchemy (Transformation)
3/11 – 15	71 HAIYAEL – Divine Warrior & Weaponry
3/16 – 20	72 MUMIAH – Endings & Rebirth

The 72 Angels' Times of Intellect Support

The following shows all 72 Angels in their one 20-minute period in the 24-hour day when they are governing the intellect plane, and thus expressing particular qualities of Divine Mind in your human intellect to help you cultivate awareness and higher-mind. Your Intellect Angel is the one that was governing 20 minutes within your time of birth. Thus, if you were born at 12:10 a.m., your Intellect Angel would be 1 VEHUIAH. Those born at a cusp time – on the hour or 20 minutes before or after – have two Intellect Angels; so if you were born at 12:20, your two Intellect Angels would be 1 VEHUIAH and 2 JELIEL. Note that because we are met by the Divine in the context of wherever we are, your Intellect Angel will be the one that was governing at your time of birth according to the place you were born. Also note that for those who use a 24-hour clock, 12 am midnight to 12 pm noon would be 00:00-12:00, and 12pm noon to 12 midnight is 12:00-24:00.

12 Midnight (a.m.) to 12 Noon (p.m.)
(00:00 – 12:00)

12:00 – 12:20 | 1 VEHUIAH – Will & New Beginnings
12:20 – 12:40 | 2 JELIEL – Love & Wisdom
12:40 – 1:00 | 3 SITAEL – Construction of Worlds
1:00 – 1:20 | 4 ELEMIAH – Divine Power
1:20 – 1:40 | 5 MAHASIAH – Rectification
1:40 – 2:00 | 6 LELAHEL – Light of Understanding
2:00 – 2:20 | 7 ACHAIAH – Patience
2:20 – 2:40 | 8 CAHETEL – Divine Blessings
2:40 – 3:00 | 9 HAZIEL – Divine Mercy & Forgiveness
3:00 – 3:20 | 10 ALADIAH – Divine Grace
3:20 – 3:40 | 11 LAUVIAH – Victory
3:40 – 4:00 | 12 HAHAIAH – Refuge/Shelter
4:00 – 4:20 | 13 YEZALEL – Fidelity, Loyalty, Allegiance
4:20 – 4:40 | 14 MEBAHEL – Truth, Liberty, Justice
4:40 – 5:00 | 15 HARIEL – Purification
5:00 – 5:20 | 16 HAKAMIAH – Loyalty
5:20 – 5:40 | 17 LAVIAH – Revelation
5:40 – 6:00 | 18 CALIEL – Justice

6:00 – 6:20 | 19 LEUVIAH – Expansive Intelligence, Fruition
6:20 – 6:40 | 20 PAHALIAH – Redemption
6:40 – 7:00 | 21 NELCHAEL – Ardent Desire to Learn
7:00 – 7:20 | 22 YEIAYEL – Fame/Renown
7:20 – 7:40 | 23 MELAHEL – Healing Capacity
7:40 – 8:00 | 24 HAHEUIAH – Protection
8:00 – 8:20 | 25 NITH-HAIAH – Spiritual Wisdom & Magic
8:20 – 8:40 | 26 HAAIAH – Political Science & Ambition
8:40 – 9:00 | 27 YERATEL – Propagation of the Light
9:00 – 9:20 | 28 SEHEIAH – Longevity
9:20 – 9:40 | 29 REIYEL – Liberation
9:40 – 10:00 | 30 OMAEL – Fertility, Multiplicity
10:00 – 10:20 | 31 LECABEL – Intellectual Talent
10:20 – 10:40 | 32 VASARIAH – Clemency & Equilibrium
10:40 – 11:00 | 33 YEHUIAH – Subordination to Higher Order
11:00 – 11:20 | 34 LEHAHIAH – Obedience
11:20 – 11:40 | 35 CHAVAKIAH – Reconciliation
11:40 – 12:00 | 36 MENADEL – Inner/Outer Work

12:00 Noon (p.m.) to 12 Midnight (a.m.)
(12:00 – 24:00)

12:00 – 12:20 | 37 ANIEL – Breaking the Circle
12:20 – 12:40 | 38 HAAMIAH – Ritual & Ceremony
12:40 – 1:00 | 39 REHAEL – Filial Submission
1:00 – 1:20 | 40 YEIAZEL – Divine Consolation & Comfort
1:20 – 1:40 | 41 HAHAHEL – Mission
1:40 – 2:00 | 42 MIKAEL – Political Authority & Order
2:00 – 2:20 | 43 VEULIAH – Prosperity
2:20 – 2:40 | 44 YELAHIAH – Karmic Warrior
2:40 – 3:00 | 45 SEALIAH – Motivation & Willfulness
3:00 – 3:20 | 46 ARIEL – Perceiver & Revealer
3:20 – 3:40 | 47 ASALIAH – Contemplation
3:40 – 4:00 | 48 MIHAEL – Fertility & Fruitfulness
4:00 – 4:20 | 49 VEHUEL – Elevation & Grandeur
4:20 – 4:40 | 50 DANIEL – Eloquence
4:40 – 5:00 | 51 HAHASIAH – Universal Medicine
5:00 – 5:20 | 52 IMAMIAH – Expiation of Errors

5:20 – 5:40	53	NANAEL – Spiritual Communication
5:40 – 6:00	54	NITHAEL – Rejuvenation & Eternal Youth
6:00 – 6:20	55	MEBAHIAH – Intellectual Lucidity
6:20 – 6:40	56	POYEL – Fortune & Support
6:40 – 7:00	57	NEMAMIAH – Discernment
7:00 – 7:20	58	YEIALEL – Mental Force
7:20 – 7:40	59	HARAHEL – Intellectual Richness
7:40 – 8:00	60	MITZRAEL – Internal Reparation
8:00 – 8:20	61	UMABEL – Affinity & Friendship
8:20 – 8:40	62	IAH– HEL – Desire to Know
8:40 – 9:00	63	ANAUEL – Perception of Unity
9:00 – 9:20	64	MEHIEL – Vivification (Invigorate/Enliven)
9:20 – 9:40	65	DAMABIAH – Fountain of Wisdom
9:40 – 10:00	66	MANAKEL – Knowledge of Good & Evil
10:00 – 10:20	67	EYAEL – Transformation to Sublime
10:20 – 10:40	68	HABUHIAH – Healing
10:40 – 11:00	69	ROCHEL – Restitution
11:00 – 11:20	70	JABAMIAH – Alchemy (Transformation)
11:20 – 11:40	71	HAIYAEL – Divine Warrior & Weaponry
11:40 – 12:00	72	MUMIAH – Endings & Rebirth

Appendix II
A Brief Summary of the 72 Angels Tradition

My first **Birth Angels** book in 2004 introduces the tradition of the 72 Angels of the Tree of Life which was said to have been systematized beginning in the 12th century by Rabbi Isaac the Blind in France, and carried forward into 13th-15th century Gerona, Spain by Rabbis, scholars and mystics working within the **Judaic Kabbalah** and other mystical traditions. I list the important influences here to give some philosophical backdrop to the Angel wisdoms: **Christian Gnosticism** (direct knowing of God through personal communion), **Sufism** (coming closer to the "inner Beloved" while still in life through love and unity-identification), **Hinduism** (the many "gods" as the many aspects of the "One Supreme Being" dwelling within and awaiting our recognition), **Neoplatonism** (espousing the "One" and the "Infinite" beyond being, from which all Life is brought forth containing the essence of the Divine One) and **Hermetics** (the Egyptian and Greek spiritual alchemy of transforming base *mettle* into the gold of wisdom and ennobled beingness in order to manifest Heaven on Earth). These spiritual pioneers of the Middle Ages and Renaissance believed in the right of all humankind – both men and women of all creeds and cultures – to have direct communion with the Divine without the dictates or exclusivity of dogma. Heretical notions for the time!

In the 13th century, a yeshiva in Gerona, Spain was founded by Talmudist and Kabbalist Rabbi Moses ben Nachman (Nachmanides), who was a disciple of Kabbalist Azriel of Girona, who himself was a disciple of Isaac the Blind. In 1492 the school and Jewish grotto were walled up and abandoned during the Conversion/Expulsion Edict of the Spanish Inquisition and remained hidden until excavations began in the 1970's of the area, now referred to as "the Call." The manuscripts that were found dealing with the 72 Angels and Tree of Life tradition are said to reveal a vibrant creation cosmology which adds Angelic detail to the ancient symbology of the Tree as a universal "flow chart" for the descent and differentiation of the Divine Oneness into the hierarchies of the 72 Angels and all of Creation. Working with the Tree of Life as a prototype for universal man, these 12th-15th century Kabbalists understood the 72 Angels as key "connectors" in the mysteries of the Divine-Human two-way relationship. As the "edible fruits" of the Tree given to humanity for ingesting the Divine and quickening our own soul essence, the Angels enable the Divine to branch out into Earth through the soul-heart-mind-body of human beingness, and the Human to return to our Divine roots inwardly through transformation and ascendance back up the Angelic Tree into higher consciousness.

People are often surprised to learn that there is no one definitive Kabbalah holy book or text. The Kabbalah was for centuries a mystical oral tradition that was practiced within, but somewhat hidden from, mainstream Judaism. It is largely based on esoteric study of ancient wisdoms, revelations, inspired texts and inner receivings passed down through the ages from Rabbis, mystics and scholars to the next generation of disciples and students. The earliest known Kabbalah work, arguably attributed to Abraham or Moses, is the *Sepher Yetzirah* ("Book of Formation"), a short but intense mystical treatise about how the utterances of the first "Creator Sounds," which ultimately became known as the Hebrew Alphabet, brought about Creation. It is the cosmology in this ancient work that Kabbalists through the ages have referred to in their understanding of the nature of the Divine and Creation.

The original *Birth Angels* book references Kabbalistic and multi-traditional sources spanning over 2500 years, as well as certain works by French mystic and scholar François Bernad-Termes, writing as Haziel, whose numerous books dealing with the Kabbalah, Angels and astrology drew from the excavated manuscripts. I was introduced to the 72 Angels tradition around 1996-97 by French Canadian and Swiss-French teachers Kaya and Christiane Muller, who work with the 72 Angels and dream symbology (www.ucm.ca/en/info/the-72-angels). Also, after *Birth Angels* was published in 2004, A.S.I.A.C.T., a color education institute associated with Aura-Soma Colour-Care Products in the U.K., developed a series of courses under the inspired guidance of Chairman Mike Booth relating the 72 Angels and the Tree of Life to their color products and consciousness-philosophies which were drawn from the inspired work of Vicky Wall, Rudolph Steiner, Goethe, Isaac Newton, Aristotle and more.

The 72 Angels tradition is compelling because there is a kind of spiritual science and ageless but exacting wisdom to it that calls us to an Angel-assisted practice of inner engagement through feeling and direct knowing rather than adherence to a particular religion or dogma. While the tradition does not espouse or exclude religion, it has the capacity to re-enliven any religion or path since it contains aspects that are in the mystical hearts of most, if not all, traditions. The foundational premise of the 72 Angels and Tree of Life tradition is that God is within us and we are within God, and both the Divine and the Human are evolving and expanding together. Perhaps most significant is that it answers some of the deepest longings and potentials we hold in our individual hearts, where the Angels do their transformational work.

Below is a brief recap of my understanding and inner experiences of the central aspects of the tradition that invite us to look at the Angels, and ourselves, in a whole new light.

The 72 Angels as the Divine within the Human

The 72 Angels are understood by Kabbalists working with the Tree of Life symbology as energetic expressions of the 72 Names, Being and Qualities of the Divine. While some thinking regards the hierarchies of Angels as created beings, the Angelic Tree of Life mysteries say that the 72 Angels are the initial *emanations* of the Divine Itself, revealing and energetically embodying the inherent diversity of Its nature. This is likely a correspondence to what some Judeo-Christian literatures call "Angels of the Presence" which came forth on the "first day" and were said to represent the faces of God, as God Itself.

In addition, as "birth-gifts" of the Divine Essence acting from within and among us, the 72 Angels illuminate and amplify the vast spectrum of possibilities and purposes within humanity, while our personal Birth Angels especially signify and support what we each are here to do, heal, express and manifest in our current lifetime. To summarize, these are the special roles of the Angels in our human lives:

As two way messengers between the Human and the Divine, they are not just carrying prayers and answers back and forth. They are transmitting Divine Essence and Energies into us, and returning what we experience in our human Earth-life to the Divine. This two-way exchange evolves and expands both the Divine and the Human.

As conveyors of the Love and Truth which compose the totality of the Divine Nature, they use our hearts to create a bridge between soul and body by broadcasting and amplifying our soul-voice and purposes within our hearts through love, compassion, intuition, heart-truth and wisdom.

As angles and amplifiers of light-consciousness, they amplify within us those qualities of the Divine which they embody and which our soul has chosen to manifest in our current lifetime through our physical, emotional and mental being and purpose.

As transformers of our base mettle into a goldenness of being, they help to heal the karma of harbored hurts and issues so that we may be free to express the dharma of our soul purposes in service to ourselves, each other and the Divine.

As expressions of the diverse nature of the Divine, the Angels illuminate for us the diversity of qualities which compose our own Divine-Human nature, as well as help us to understand that *it takes the totality of humankind and the beings and things of the natural world and beyond to reveal and express the diverse nature of God*. This suggests the importance of not just tolerating each other's diversities, but embracing ourselves and all beings, ways and things as valuable and illuminating pieces of the bigger picture puzzle of the Divine and Life Itself. Truly, we are each here to literally "flesh out" our part of the picture with the fullness of our unique being – for ourselves, each other and the fullness of the Divine on Earth.

* * *

For more detail about the 72 Angels tradition, see *Birth Angels ~ Fulfilling Your Life Purpose with the 72 Angels of the Kabbalah* and Vol. 1 of *Birth Angels Book of Days*. (TerahCox.com & Amazon.com)

BIRTH ANGELS BOOK OF DAYS
Daily Wisdoms with the 72 Angels of the Tree of Life

Volume 1: March 21 – June 2
Relationship with the Divine

Volume 2: June 3 – August 16
Relationship with Self

Volume 3: August 17 – October 29
Relationship with Work and Purpose

Volume 4: October 30 – January 8
Relationship with Others

Volume 5: January 9 – March 20
Relationship with Community and the World

Additional Offerings
Quick-Reference Charts & Posters: The Kabbalistic Tree of Life
72 Angels of the Tree of Life ~ Days & Hours of Governing
Birth Angels Meditation Cards
Speaking, Personal Coaching & Workshops
www.TerahCox.com

*You are invited to share your experiences
in working with the 72 Angels
by contacting the author at*
HeavenandEarthWorks@gmail.com

About the Author

TERAH COX has worked with the Kabbalah, Christianity, Sufism and other spiritual traditions and wisdoms throughout her life in search of the common threads of Love and Truth in their mystical hearts. She is the author of *The Story of Love & Truth, Birth Angels ~ Fulfilling Your Life Purpose with the 72 Angels of the Kabbalah, You Can Write Song Lyrics*, the five-volume series of *Birth Angels Book of Days* and several works in progress. She is also a speaker, coach and mentor on the subjects of individuation and life purposing, creativity, diversity/unity and spiritual development.

Formerly a writer for the Aura-Soma Colour-Care-System® in the U.K., she was also signed to the music publishing companies of Columbia Pictures, BMG Music, Warner-Chappell and various European music publishers as a lyric writer of over 150 songs recorded for CDs, film and television. Her poetry-art designs for wall-art, greeting cards, prints and more are online and in galleries and retail shops across the U.S.

* * *

Books, speaking, coaching and workshops
www.TerahCox.com

Original greeting cards, prints, word-art & books
www.HeavenandEarthWorks.com

E-Cards with original music, messages and art
www.MilestonesConnect.com

TERAH COX

9001143R00139

Printed in Great Britain
by Amazon.co.uk, Ltd.,
Marston Gate.